DUST-OFF

Al smashed into the top of a tree, and the bottom of the cockpit bubble shattered, showering the VC below with tiny pieces of Plexiglas. The chopper banked sharply to the left and limped along as quickly as Al could coax it. In minutes he was able to straighten it out in a level attitude.

The VC were behind them, and Al aimed the big bird at a long dirt road to his left front. He banked right as he reached the road and traveled directly over it.

The medic screamed, and Al turned his head, as did Robbie, who was helping the medic attend to the wounded. Beyond the medic, Al saw that a wounded soldier had fallen out the door and was half-sitting, half-lying on the starboard skid.

"Don't let go, buddy!" Al yelled. "We're going to save you."

Also by Don Bendell:

THE B-52 OVERTURE
VALLEY OF TEARS

SNAKE-EATER

*Characters in
and stories about the
U.S. Army Special Forces
in the Vietnam War*

DON BENDELL

A DELL BOOK

Published by
Dell Publishing
a division of
Bantam Doubleday Dell Publishing Group, Inc.
1540 Broadway
New York, New York 10036

ISBN: 0-440-21141-7

Printed in the United States of America
Published simultaneously in Canada
May 1994
10 9 8 7 6 5 4 3 2 1
OPM

Acknowledgment

This book is dedicated to all the men and women who are Vietnam veterans. You did what you believed in, but many chastised you for doing it. You won all the battles, but they wouldn't let you win the war. Some of you were left behind and forgotten by those who sent you, but you'll never be forgotten by those of us who served with you. If you are a Vietnam veteran, stand tall, and be proud. You were, and are, the very best of America's sons and daughters. We all suffer some degree of PTSD, but we all can look ourselves in the eye when we face the mirror each day, smile and wink, and find the courage to go on living in a peaceful world.

LEGACY OF A GREEN BERET

The years have now passed since I wore it with pride,
That "badge of distinction" for which some friends died.
Only three in a hundred earned their beret,
Through hard work and study and sweat every day.

I walked among warriors with scalps on my belt.
My words were of iron, and what strength I felt.
My heart was like flint and my face made of stone,
And in a large crowd, I stood out all alone.

My word's still my bond, and my mind is still set.
They think me quite strange some of those that I've met.
The toughest of men would not stand in my way,
Because of green felt on my head, my beret.

The girls sometimes blushed and some men bought me
*   beers,*
And with my false pride, I was scared to shed tears.
I fought with such passion but loved with it, too;
And wrapped myself up in the red, white, and blue.

That hat told the world, I was one of the best,
I don't wear it now, or my past on my chest,
But now in my heart I still wear my beret,
For inside, I'm SF, till my dying day.

There's so many lessons I've learned through the years.
I got them through laughter and heartache and tears.
One lesson I learned, which I now understand,
It's not what I wear which then makes me a man.

1

Third Herd

A LOT WAS HAPPENING in early 1970. My A-camp back in 'Nam, Detachment A-242, Dak Pek, was overrun by the NVA. Many, many friends were killed or captured. Commo Willy and Master Sergeant Tom Weeks got out alive, along with a few others. Like most Green Berets, they didn't just *leave* Dak Pek; they left as heroes. The NVA may have taken the camp, but they knew the U.S. Army Special Forces had been there. Weeks, the team sergeant, had called in massive air strikes, including a B-52 carpet bombing strike, while they were still in the camp. He also hosed down three NVA who were trying to hoist a North Vietnamese flag up the flagpole on the camp parade ground—if you could call it that. It was actually the only flat spot with no trees that could host a volleyball game in the whole valley of the Dak Poko River.

Every week, I requested a chance to go back to Vietnam, and every week I heard the same response: "Captain Bendell, I'm sorry. You have a 'three' medical profile. You are not going back to Vietnam."

Not long before, I was supposed to be Officer of the Day for JFK Special Warfare Center. Of course, the name had been changed in those days to appease the antiwar protesters—it was called the JFK Center for Military Assistance.

I hated my job at Fort Bragg. It was a desk job. I

begged the S-1 to schedule me for any operation that came up as long as I could get out in the boonies, the home of every true SFer.

What a dream. Just when I thought I would die from terminal boredom, I came into work one day and was told, "Captain, go home and get your jungle gear. You're going out in the field."

On my way home and back to Fort Bragg, there was no singing along with James Brown or my other heroes. I just kept saying things like "Thank you, God" over and over.

Later that morning, I was loaded onto an old World War II–vintage C-47 with another captain, a lieutenant, and ten NCOs—an A-team. We were all issued MC-1 parachutes, which were steerable T-10s, reserve chutes, and aviator kit bags.

I walked up to the NCO in charge of our excursion from Bragg to Pope AFB. "What's the story, Top? Where we going?" I asked.

"Can't tell you, sir," he replied. "I can only tell you that you are accompanying this team as a judge. You guys are being dropped in somewhere and will be told on the drop zone where you are and what your orders are."

I handed him a Lucky and lit one myself. Grinning, I said, "We get to shoot anybody?"

He laughed. "Spoken like a true snake-eater," he said.

He saluted and I returned it, watching him, still laughing, climb into the shotgun seat of the deuce-and-a-half truck that hauled us to Pope.

I turned and started to load into the old C-47.

A young E-5 ahead of me said, "Shit, sir. We have to ride somewhere in this old piece of shit?"

He took a "honey pot" from the Air Force crew chief and set it in the back of the craft.

Holding up the parachute, I replied, "Don't bitch, Sergeant. At least we get to jump out of this thing. These poor fuckers have to *land* in it."

The Air Force crew chief laughed heartily, shaking his head from side to side.

The navigator on the old aircraft pulled out his maps and charts and tried to figure out what route would have the most turbulence and worst storms. When he figured it out, that was where we flew.

"Where are we?" I asked.

The crew chief smiled and shrugged. "Sorry, sir."

After telling the team we had five minutes, I asked, "How's the drop zone marked?"

"Panels," he said. "And your rendezvous on the ground will have a smoke going."

I was to jump-master the drop. The portside door was opened, and I looked at the static line running diagonally across the aircraft. The door was too small to shuffle up to, crouch down, and leap out as in most planes. The men would really have to crouch low before jumping, since the door was so small. The red light next to the door was on. I looked out and felt extreme heat as the prop wash blasted me in the face. Wherever we were was even hotter and more humid than North Carolina.

I faced the team and gave them a hand signal, then yelled, "Get ready!"

Next I yelled, "Stand up!"

The team all stood, holding the snap link attached to their static lines in their left hands.

I gave a hook signal with my finger. "Hook up!" I yelled.

They hooked the links to the diagonal line and still held the yellow static lines in their left hands.

"Check equipment!"

Everyone checked their equipment, while I scanned everything I could think of.

"Check static lines!" I yelled.

The team members, from the second one back, checked the static lines of the ones in front of them, and the last turned so the one in front of him could check his. I looked out the door and saw smoke swirling up ahead through a lot of trees. Below, I saw a two-lane paved road and more trees, with occasional little bare meadows with cows grazing.

The crew chief gave me a nod and a wink.

I smiled, pointed, and yelled, "Stand in the door!"

The whole team shuffled along the aircraft, very bent over. The first guy on the team, the radio operator, stood in the door of the plane, his left foot forward, his hands holding the outside of the aircraft. My eyes were glued on the little red light just beyond his head. The light went off, and the green one came on.

"Go!" I hollered, and he leaped up and out into space.

The whole team did the same, rapidly following the first one out into the hot sky. I followed the last one out the door and felt as if I had jumped right into a giant blast furnace. My elbow was sticking out from my side, so when my chute opened, I tried to raise my head up to check it out, but couldn't. Since my elbow stuck out a little, the prop blast spun me like a top while the canopy deployed.

I reached up with both hands and felt the thick green risers that connected to all the nylon suspension lines. I pulled on the risers and bicycle-kicked my legs. I started spinning and was soon untangled, hanging below a fully inflated canopy. Looking down at what was supposed to be our drop zone, I saw more cows grazing in a meadow, which was dotted with clusters of trees.

Shit, I thought. SF. Do they always have to drop us in trees?

Even at Fort Bragg we had to jump on St. Mere Eglise Drop Zone, which was the smallest and cruddiest of all the post's DZs. The Eighty-Deuce jumped on Normandy and the other big sandy drop zones.

We didn't drop very far and the wind was barely blowing, so I didn't pull the pins on my harness, which would have enabled me to turn and steer the MC-1 easier. I saw several men hit the ground and/or trees. I pulled on my left front and back rear risers, spinning my chute around so I was facing the wind. The MC-1 parachute has a gore out of the back of the canopy that is used for steering, giving the chute an eight-knot-per-hour forward movement. The wind was blowing at about eight knots, so I floated almost straight down. I looked at the horizon and put my feet and knees together preparing for a good PLF (parachute landing fall).

"Fuck it," I said at the last second, and spread my legs, looking at the ground.

I hit on the balls of my feet and took two quick steps forward doing a stand-up landing. I collapsed my canopy.

Zip Zepeda, an E-7 who was the team operation sergeant, came up behind me, a broad smile on his face. "Trying for a court-martial, huh, Captain?"

"Fuck no, Sergeant," I replied in the common jargon of Special Forces. "I didn't do a stand-up landing. I did a proper PLF, but the wind blew me back up."

Zip started laughing as I S-rolled my canopy over my arms and stuffed it into the aviator kit bag. I grabbed all my gear, and we walked side by side toward a deuce-and-a-half and master sergeant at the edge of the wannabe drop zone. Several team members were already there at the turn-in point.

"Where the hell are we, Zip?" I asked.

"Beats the shit outta me, Captain," he replied. "But it's hotter than Bragg. I know that."

We met with the rendezvous NCO and checked in our chutes and reserves, which was supposed to simulate cacheting them.

He handed the operation order to the team commander, a bespectacled captain with prematurely graying hair. He called me to the side and introduced himself, as did I.

"Where in the hell am I, Sergeant?" I asked.

He grinned broadly and lit a Pall Mall. "Tiger Ridge, Louisiana, *Dai-uy,*" he said. "We're about forty miles north of Fort Polk. Buncha new-birds, they call them, just finished AIT and are gonna get shipped to 'Nam as replacements in grunt units. The team's supposed to be VC and operate against them in the woods around here, so they can find out what it's all about. You're to judge their performance."

I felt rivers of sweat running down my rib cage, chest, and back, as if I were back in Vietnam. The miserable feeling was comforting in a weird sense. It is, I suppose, kind of like a person who grows up as a victim of abuse, then feels they are receiving love or attention only when they suffer further abuse.

Within hours, as good SFers always do, the A-team I was to judge found the thickest, wettest, most impenetrable part of the swamps in the area and located our guerrilla base there. We all carried jungle gear and set up hammocks between trees with poncho canopies overhead. It was to be our home for the next several weeks. Thank God for desk jobs in SF, I thought.

The team radio operator brought an AN-GRC/109, or Angry 109, radio with a hand-cranked generator. He cut an antenna and strung it in the trees. He immediately started trying to reach Fort Bragg with his CW capability. The assistant radio operator, in the meantime, did what all good assistants do in such circumstances: He wore his arms out cranking the generator. Of all the men on the team, only the senior radio operator carried live ammunition for his weapon, an Army Colt .45 automatic pistol. He carried with him a code pad for transmitting messages, which had an intelligence rating of "confidential"; hence the loaded pistol.

The first day, two men were sent to a nearby bridge spanning a two-rut dirt road over a stream, the lowest drainage point for the swamp we were in. The two young sergeants returned carrying a very large poisonous cottonmouth snake without its head.

They proudly held the snake up, and one said, "Lunchtime."

Zip Zepeda and I grinned at each other and raised our eyes. He was also a Vietnam vet, having served with Fifth Group, too. It never failed—every time I ever went out "in the field" with SF, some young trooper or officer had to try to live up to the nickname "snake-eater" that had been given to SF years before. While I was a second lieutenant with the Seventh Group in '67 and early '68, I did the same thing—offering up a large copperhead I had killed. I'm sure the more experienced officers and NCOs there also smiled and raised their eyes while my back was turned.

It's been said that rattlesnake tastes like sweet chicken, and it's true—some do. But some don't, and they taste quite gamey. I've also eaten copperhead, cottonmouth, and python and hated the taste. In fact, when the two young buck sergeants started skinning the cotton-

mouth out to broil it for lunch, Zip and I broke out two
packs of C-rations.

"Nothing like a good meal of old cardboard when
some guys are trying to play John Wayne, huh?" I said.

"You got it, Cappin'," he replied.

After the evening meal, Zip told a couple of the young
NCOs to bury the day's trash really deep, near the base
camp. That night, in the black of the swamp and the dark
of the night sky, we heard a shadow pass among our hammocks. It wound its way between each man and went
straight to the trash grave, and we heard much sniffing. It
started ripping the trash out of the ground with its powerful front paws.

I whispered, "I thought bears in the wild were supposed to be scared shitless of humans."

Zip whispered back, "This son of a bitch forgot to
read the book about black bear behavior."

The senior radio operator said, "Is anybody out of
your hammock?"

Nobody answered.

"Stay where you are," he said. "I'm going to blast the
fucker."

There were three shots, and the bear disappeared into
the swamp while a pair of flashlight beams followed him.

I noticed that the team commander, the captain, had
no leadership abilities whatsoever. The XO, recently pro-
moted to first lieutenant, and Zip Zepeda ran everything.
It even got to the point where they told the captain what
was going to happen, and he would just smile and nod his
head. I made a mental note to write a report to the "old
man" commending Zepeda and the young officer for their
outstanding leadership.

After the first week, I asked the captain if I could

speak to him. He grinned and nodded. I didn't really want that conversation, but it had to occur.

"Captain," I said, looking him in the eyes, which is the SF way, "you have date-of-rank on me, but I have been assigned to grade and judge the performance of your team. I think you're a nice guy, but that's also part of the problem for you. When we return to Bragg, I'm going to write a report to your CO suggesting that you be transferred to a different unit because your leadership ability is weak—very weak. I think there's bound to be a place for you somewhere, but it cannot be in Special Forces. I'm sorry, but I don't feel you should be wearing a beret, especially in combat. I hate telling you this, but I have to—I don't do things like this behind someone's back."

His smile was gone, but it came back as he spoke. "Captain Bendell, I understand," he said. "Maybe you're right. I know I'm real meek."

I didn't know what to say, so I simply replied, "I'm not a fucking shrink, Captain. I can only tell you, if you want to be a commander in SF, get some balls. Find them somewhere, and then act like you've got them. It's simple as that. Good luck."

I stuck my hand out to shake, expecting, maybe even hoping he'd punch me, but he shook, smiled meekly, and retired to his jungle hammock.

That night, he stayed at the base camp as Zip and the gung-ho young lieutenant led the team on a night patrol. We were on our way to the company's perimeter when a pair of headlights appeared around the bend in the road we followed. We ran into the trees and hid behind trees and bushes.

As I knelt behind a large oak tree, I heard a rattling sound directly in front of my own balls. I jumped and felt something slam into my knee. The night, especially the thick woods, was pitch black. The headlights were almost upon us, and I knew that, as a judge, I could not compromise this team in any way, shape, or form.

I froze in place. "Don't anybody move," I said. "I just got bit on the kneecap by a rattler."

I felt a shadow move up beside me and heard the footsteps. The lights passed: an enemy deuce-and-a-half.

A flashlight came on at my elbow, and I saw the snake strike at the M-16 barrel poking at it. The fangs locked around the flash suppressor, and Zip Zepeda's M-16 blank round blew the deadly snake's head off. Zip picked up the body, and the team gathered around examining it.

Zip said, "Captain, it was a copperhead, not a rattler. All poisonous snakes will shake their tails when they're nervous, and this guy rattled his against the little sapling you knelt beside."

"Let me check out my knee."

I quickly dropped my jungle fatigue pants and looked. Apparently, the snake's nose or mouth had hit my knee, but somehow the fangs hadn't. As in Vietnam many times, I was once again protected, by God—and by a Special Forces NCO.

An hour later, we infiltrated the company perimeter and attacked the grunts with smoke grenades, blanks, artillery simulators, and other pyrotechnics, one of which exploded directly in front of my face, blinding me. I wasn't able to see for about an hour, and the trainees were hot on our heels. It wouldn't have mattered, had I been captured, that I was just a referee: I wore a green beret. Fortunately, so did the NCOs I was with, and two of them grabbed my arms and guided me, running full speed through the thick black woods.

Once again, my ass was being covered by SF sergeants. I thought of Zip rushing to my side in the darkness to protect me from a poisonous snake. I thought of my talk with the captain, who did get shipped out to a leg unit when we returned to Bragg. I thought of all the incidents I survived in Vietnam. All of this reminded me of one thing that Master Sergeant Mike "Hardcore" Holland told me in Seventh Group in '67.

He said, "Lieutenant, you're working with the best NCOs in the whole fucking world. If you're an asshole or know-it-all, they won't frag you. They'll stand up to your face and slit your fucking throat, with all due respect, sir. If you listen to their experience and advice and provide a little leadership, they'll respect you, keep you alive, and make you look good."

Mike Holland was right. I thought about all the various characters I had met and would meet in Special Forces. I had met sergeants with master's degrees, even doctorates. These men were the best-trained, most highly motivated, most dangerous fighting force the world had ever seen. I worked with men who had been mercenaries in every war in the world, men who had infiltrated foreign countries and successfully completed sabotage operations, warriors who had been tortured and held in prisons in Cuba, Africa, the Middle East, South America, and North Vietnam, soldiers who had risked their lives to secretly put out numerous little fires around the world before they became blazing flames of war. With a group like that, there are bound to be some real characters, and there were, but every damned one of them was a hero, a true American hero.

2

Sneaky Petes

SERGEANT MAJOR AL FONTES was the "team daddy" of Heavy Hook Bravo Team for MAC-V/SOG at a secret forward operating base in Thailand in 1969. At the time, everything he and everyone in the unit did was classified top secret. MAC-V/SOG was an acronym for Military Advisory Command–Vietnam/Studies and Observation Group. In actuality, that was a soft-sounding name for a top secret unit composed almost exclusively of U.S. Special Forces personnel, along with the best mercenary fighters money could buy, mainly of the Montagnard and Chinese Nung variety. The pilots who worked with the teams were United States–trained Vietnamese pilots with brass balls. All the complaints made by SF personnel about the cowardice of Vietnamese ARVN soldiers were forgotten when they witnessed the SOG chopper pilots in action. I had the same feelings about VN pilots after seeing a pair of them in A1E Skyraiders put in an air strike for me in 1968 that saved my butt big-time. The SOG pilots were further hampered by the fact that they mainly used old choppers that should have been mothballed years before.

SOG teams had many different missions, but all of them were dangerous. Six- to nine-man RTs, or recon teams, were usually inserted into an area in Laos, Cambodia, or North Vietnam. A team usually consisted of two Americans and the rest indigenous personnel. They would be sent in on "snatch missions," or missions to capture a prisoner to update current intelligence; other direct action–type missions such as sabotaging enemy ammunition supplies or weapons; manning radio relay sites; or just plain old recon missions.

Many times, a team calling for extraction would be "hot," and a hatchet force, about a platoon-size unit of ass-kickers, would be sent in to help them get out of the "hot area." Other methods of extraction for SOG RTs were Stabo or McGuire rigs suspended from helicopters, or even Operation Black Knife or Sky Hook. A pack would be dropped containing a suit attached to a long tether. The nylon-webbed tether line was attached to a helium-filled miniblimp, which would rise into the sky a couple hundred feet and hold the line straight up in the air. The suit had a reserve parachute attached to the abdomen. The person being extracted would put on the suit and then sit on the ground with legs crossed and head down while the balloon held the line aloft above him.

A specially equipped C-130 Hercules aircraft would fly overhead. The C-130 had a device on its nose with two prongs sticking out like a giant V that made the plane look like it had catfish whiskers. Below the miniblimp, the line would be marked with two little flags, and the plane would hit the line right between the flags. The device at the plane's nose grabbed the line and transferred it to the rear of the plane, attaching it to an electronic winch. At the same time, the balloon was cut free. The person wearing the suit would be jerked off the ground, right up through trees sometimes, and be winched into the tailgate of the plane as it flew away.

Teams in SOG had the best equipment and supplies available—except for the main tool they used for extraction and insertion, and that was the old beat-up CH-34 chopper, with a brass-balled VN pilot driving it. The pilots' and crew members' courage, along with their ability to fix a broken chopper blade with adhesive tape or maybe patch a bullet hole in the skin with used chewing gum, made up for the lack of equipment in the helicopter department. All the guns that RTs carried and their equipment, clothing, and ammunition were completely "sterile." Nothing, not even the matchbooks, said "Made in the USA." Because of the *top* secret classification of the unit, other commanders or staff people could not enter SOG compounds around the country, not even generals.

Teams from CCN, CCC, and CCS—Command and Control North, Central, and South—working in Laos, Cambodia, and North Vietnam would sometimes fly into Thailand at night on Blackbird aircraft: top secret Air Force C-123s and C-130s that were painted black and were also sterile. They were supplied by the First Tactical Air Wing of the USAF. The teams would land after dark, and Al Fontes would have several black vans, with imitation U.S. Embassy license plates on them, back up to the off-ramps of the planes. The RT members went right from the plane into the van and were whisked away to a barracks. Al had made a deal with the NCO club manager for nice meals of steaks and other goodies to be served. The man never knew what they were for, but he knew they were doing somebody important some good, so he helped out.

The commander of Heavy Hook Bravo Team was Lieutenant Colonel "Pappy" Shelton.

Al instituted an SOP that required all team members to take turns riding on VR—visual reconnaissance—missions. They would ride out over the countryside of Laos or Cambodia in an O-1 prop-driven aircraft with an Air Force FAC, or forward air controller, to locate good landing zones, or LZs, to insert teams into an area.

Taking his turn flying VR on one occasion, Al Fontes was scouting for a good LZ to insert an RT, which waited back at the FOB to get the word. As usual, they were in a CH-34 chopper with a clang-while-he-walked VN pilot driving. The team had a mission to locate, recon, and report on a large NVA unit that was headquartered in that general area. Al saw some signs of recent activity and found a likely LZ where he could insert the team.

Master Sergeant James Sweeney was manning the commo room at the forward operating base, or FOB. His call sign was "Jimbo," and Al's was "Coyote."

"Jimbo, this is Coyote. Over," Al said into the radio mike.

"Jimbo here. Go. Over," Sweeney answered.

Al said simply, "Got a bingo. Over!"

"Roger. Out."

When Sweeney got the phrase to launch the waiting team, he sent them up into the blast furnace called the sky in the CH-34. Until the team's chopper arrived, Al and his FAC slowly circled the area around the LZ. When the big bird appeared, the FAC made a lazy circle, banked to the left, and fired a rocket into a cleared-off area in the midst of a bunch of rubber trees.

The CH-34 chopper headed straight for the white smoke swirling up from the white phosphorous marking rocket.

As the chopper descended, Al headed back toward his house in the O-1. But he was stopped after five minutes when he got a call that the LZ was "hot" and the team in serious trouble.

"This is Coyote," Al said. "Pick up the team. They're hot. Over."

The FAC turned to Al and said, "I have a couple of jets on station."

"Fucking-A," Al replied enthusiastically, "let's smoke those bastards."

The FAC grinned, winked, and banked the plane to the right.

Al got a call from the team leader on the ground: "Coyote, we're taking automatic-weapons and heavy small-arms from the other side of the LZ. Over."

"No sweat. Got some fast-movers standing by," Al replied, referring to F-4A Phantom jets. "Duck your pretty little heads while we mark the position. Over."

"Wilco. Out," the reply crackled over the radio.

The FAC fired another marking round into the LZ and told the jet pilots that the team was on the south side of the smoke and the bad guys on the north. He and Al took off and circled out far over the valley, while the quick guys did their deadly thing. They pounded the NVA with several tons of ordnance and fired them up with twenty-mike-mike cannon fire.

By the time the jets made their final pass over the target, the extraction chopper arrived, along with a hatchet force in a couple more CH-34s in case they had to go into the fight and raise some hell. They didn't. The jets had presented a convincing argument for strategic withdrawal. Excuse me—"strategic withdrawal" is what the U.S. Army does. The enemy *retreats*. They did indeed do that, and at quite a rapid pace. The chopper went down, picked them up, and headed back for home.

The team leader spotted Al's O-1 still circling but moving back toward the LZ as they headed home. "Coyote, you going home? Over," he called.

Al answered simply, "Bravo Delta Alpha, over."

The team leader said, "Rog-O, understand. Careful. Out."

He understood that Al was going back to the LZ to make a bomb damage assessment, or BDA, of the target.

Al and the FAC talked about previous battles, as the little plane banked sharply; it banked once again, then dived down at the clearing. Little fires and lots of smoke coming out of the ground and trees at various spots gave the whole area a weird look. It reminded Al of a prehistoric forest with various volcanic hot holes. They spotted a number of khaki-clad NVA bodies strewn under the trees.

The O-1 banked and swung back around, making a wide lazy circle over the LZ, while the two warriors traded comments about the destruction wrought by the pair of F-4As.

"That ought to do it," Al said. "Let's go home, Major."

The Air Force pilot gave Al a nod but said, "Why don't we take one last swing, Top, and check out that thick jungle north of the Lima Zulu?"

"Sure, why not?"

They flew in a wide circle South of the LZ, then west, and banked across the north of the smoking clearing. Al strained his eyes at the dark emerald carpet below, looking for evidence of more NVA activity. The sun had just started to slip below the distant jungle-covered mountains to the west. Al saw some little flashes down below to the right front of the aircraft. Less than a second later, several bullets tore into the bottom of the O-1 aircraft, and the engine faltered. At the same time, a bright tracer flashed past Al's window.

"Fuck," the pilot said, as Al heard the front engine sputter. "We're going down."

Al chuckled. " 'Hey come on, Top, why don't we just make one more pass over the Lima Zulu? How about it, huh?' "

The pilot laughed nervously. "Fuck you very much, you fucking snake-eater," he said. Getting serious, he continued, "We'll head as far away from here as we can with our lights out."

"Great," Al said cheerfully. "How about Pasadena? Think we can make Pasadena?"

The pilot laughed again as he held the controls and watched the altimeter dropping.

Al bent forward, his head pushing against the instrument panel. He could no longer hear the steady drone of the front and rear propellers whirring through the hot, humid air over Laos. He grunted a little as he pushed with his forehead.

The FAC pilot gave him a quizzical sidelong glance. "Fontes, what the hell are you doing?"

Al laughed. "Trying to bend over and kiss my ass good-bye, sir," he replied.

The two men laughed heartily all the way to the ground. The plane careened off a dike between two rice paddies and skipped along the water of the second paddy like a stone on a pond surface thrown by a little boy. It spun around three times and plowed through another dike and up into the air into the tops of a grove of trees. A tree trunk tore through the plane's bottom and bashed the pilot's leg, breaking it in three places. He let out a loud moan of pain. Al permanently imprinted his fingerprints into the panel in front of him as the plane flipped upside down and pancaked onto the ground.

When the aircraft came to a full stop, a loud clang was heard, followed by complete silence except for the heavy breathing of the two warriors. They both unhooked their seat belts and slid into upright positions. The pilot was white-faced. Al shook the cobwebs out of his brain, and when he got his head clear, he grabbed the pilot under his arm and helped him through the now-open doorway of the little aircraft. He wanted to get both of them away from the plane in case of fire or explosion.

They made it far enough away from the aircraft to be safe, and they stopped. Al elevated the pilot's good leg, then wrapped a poncho liner around him to keep him warm and prevent him from going into shock.

Al pulled his radio mike out and called MSG Sweeney, who was actually the senior FAC rider on the team. Sweeney knew more about VRs than anyone else in the compound, and he was well aware of what could happen on them. Twenty or thirty years after the Vietnam War ended, Sweeney figured that many of the MIA/POWs would be Air Force pilots, MAC-V/SOG, and Fifth Special Forces Group personnel. He was right.

Al said quietly, "Jimbo, I'm in big trouble. Over."

No response.

Al lifted the transmitter to his lips again when Sweeney's voice crackled over the phone: "On the way, Top."

That was it. Nothing else had to be said. Sweeney had figured out what had happened to Al and knew what direction to head. Right now, it was necessary to maintain radio silence so that searching NVA troops would have a harder time finding Al and the pilot.

Al sighed. He knew that Sweeney would send someone right away. They would maintain radio silence until they were close, and then he would turn on his blue strobe light.

What Al did not know, however, was that Sweeney himself was on his way. Right now he was in an O-1, while a CH-34 chopper piloted by Cowboy, the ballsiest of the VN pilots, followed behind by several minutes.

Al's pilot started moaning and mumbling, and every once in a while, he let out with a cry of pain. So Al pulled a morphine syrette out of his tiger suit fatigue shirt pocket. He jabbed the needle through the pilot's trouser leg and into the thigh. It wasn't long before the pilot was resting easy, and Al heard the distant drone of a plane.

He had shut down his radio entirely to save on the batteries, but he now turned it on, and instantly Sweeney's voice crackled over the airwaves.

"Coyote, Coyote, this is Jimbo. Can you hear me? Over" came the sweet-sounding familiar voice.

Al keyed his mike two times, and Sweeney said, "Give me a strobe. Over."

Al now saw the approaching O-1 aircraft. He pulled his strobe light out and flipped it on, pointing the flashing blue light toward the plane, and held his breath.

The voice crackled again: "Got you. Over."

Al replied, "Driver's got a broken leg. Over."

Referring to the helicopter, Sweeney said, "Butterfly's standing by. Drinks will be on me. Over."

Al grinned. "Roger. Out."

He lit up a cigarette and unconsciously cupped it in his hand to hide the little red embers while he waited for the chopper to arrive. He smiled and said a little silent prayer, thanking God for letting him be in Special Forces.

As he waited, Al laughed to himself and thought back to an incident seven years earlier, on his first journey to Vietnam.

It had been 1962, and Al, then an E-7, a sergeant first class, was the sergeant of a team that had traveled to 'Nam from Bravo Company with First Group in Okinawa. They established the A-camp at Cheo Reo. It was A-213, and the team members started building trust with the Jarai tribe of Montagnards who inhabited the area. Along with the Rade, Bahnar, and Kaho, the Jarai were one of the biggest of the thirty-one distinctive Montagnard tribes. They got along well with the American Green Berets and really respected them.

In fact, a year earlier the Jarai, along with the Rade, had been the biggest supporters of the new Montagnard resistance movement called the FLHPM, the Front de Libération des Hauts Plateaux-Montagnard. The first resistance movement, the BAJARAKA, was its forerunner, founded in 1958 under the leadership of a Rade named Y Bham Enuol. The name was an acronym taken from the first two letters of the names of the four largest tribes. The FLHPM was also headed by Y Bham, as was the joint trilateral resistance front called the FULRO, standing for Fronts Unifiés de Lutte des Races-Oprimées, meaning the Fronts Unified for the Liberation of the Racially Oppressed. This included the Cambodian resistance movement, the Front de Libération-Kambuja Krom, or FLKK. There was also the Cham's resistance movement called the Front de Libération-Champa, or FLC. These two fronts were headed by Um Savath and Les Kosem, who chose Y Bham to head the overall resistance organization.

The FLHPM wanted to fight to stop the discrimination levied against the Montagnard tribespeople by the Vietnamese, who were very jealous of the noble, family-oriented lifestyle of the proud and simple primitive mountain villagers. The Jarai, along with the other major tribes, supplied most of the warriors for the secret resistance movement, and the bulk of these came from the village of Cheo Reo, where Al and his team were establishing an A-camp, A-213.

As was the SOP with most A-teams, the team members at A-213 took turns going out with the Montagnard mercenaries on operations and patrols. In the normal routine two Americans and two Luc Luong Dac Biet (LLDB) or Vietnamese Special Forces personnel went on the larger operations. These operations usually covered a certain blocked-off area within that particular A-team's TAOR, or tactical area of operations. The large contingent would go out and operate in that area usually for ten days to two weeks and execute search-and-destroy missions, or reconnaissance-in-force, or set up perimeters and send out smaller patrols and ambushes to interdict enemy troop movements.

It was during one of these large operations that Al Fontes had fallen victim to the enemy in a way that didn't often happen. In fact, many SFers who heard about Al's experience said that it was "the shittiest thing that could happen."

In actuality, the whole team had been operating out of Ban Me Thuot, a major Montagnard population center. Home primarily to the Rade tribe, it also had a large contingent of Jarai. The A-team split into two groups, with one occupying the new site at Cheo Reo and the rest back in the city. The team members took turns going to Cheo Reo and going out on patrols and operations.

On this particular occasion, Al had gone out in the boonies along with the team's engineer/demolition specialist, George Foreman, from High Point, North Carolina. SF engineer/demo men are a rare breed. These guys love to make things explode and scatter into little pieces, but they also know how to expertly build bridges, buildings, and other structures out of whatever is at hand, wherever they are.

The operation had been out in the jungle for several days on a reconnaissance-in-force operation and were sweeping a large valley several klicks from the A-213 A-site. Like most SF-led patrols, they stopped every hour for a ten-minute "smoke break," primarily to have a cigarette, remove the numerous blood-filled leeches from their calves and necks, and drink a lot of water in the oven-hot, humid jungle.

During one such break, Al decided, or actually nature decided for him, that he had to quickly relieve his body of a great deal of waste products. This was a very common occurrence for American soldiers serving in Vietnam. Just about everyone took a little Dapsone pill once a week supposedly to ward off falciparum malaria and a giant Chloriquin Primiquin pill to prevent vivax malaria. Most SFers referred to the latter pill as the "horse pill" because of its monstrous size. It also was notorious for causing the constant bouts of diarrhea.

Such was the case with Al Fontes, who now pulled his tiger suit trousers down around his ankles and hung his agonized ass over a log. He smiled as he felt waves of discomfort leave his body, but he gulped when his eyes fixed on the Jarai CIDG strikers. Normally laughing and joking with each other as they relaxed, these wiry little men had suddenly stopped talking and were now holding their rifles at the ready, looking about very cautiously.

Like other "sneaky petes," Al had learned early on that Montagnard warriors somehow had a sixth sense that warned them when the enemy was nearby.

He wanted desperately to pull up his trousers, but his body wouldn't allow it. Then he heard the sound he dreaded: a hollow thud.

"Oh, fuck," he said with a gulp and a moan.

On the hilltop due east of Al's operation, a small Vietnamese man had shinnied up a thin tree, using its sporadic branches as ladder rungs. The lookout had watched Al's company-size operation pass through a small clearing and into a large patch of triple-canopy jungle. Down below the tree, five other Vietnamese men, all in black cotton pajamas, moved a base plate and 82-millimeter mortar into position. They looked up at their lookout and listened for his signal. He waited for the operation to appear in the next clearing, but it didn't. The lookout whispered and gave hand signals to the men down below, and they readied the mortar to fire. The patrol leader held one round in his left hand and another at the top of the mortar tube with his right. He dropped the round as he ducked his head down below the end of the tube. The other patrol members followed suit.

The round hit the bottom of the tube and shot out with a metallic thud sound. Down below, Al Fontes said, "Oh, fuck."

Al counted the hang time and desperately tried to push out the remaining goblins that had invaded his bowels and were holding him unmercifully to that spot. Sweat broke out on his tanned forehead as he waited for the explosive round to hit. He pictured it arcing through the hot, wet sky, and he wondered if it would hit on his make-shift toilet. Anyone who has been in the battlefield with an indirect-fire weapon being fired at them when they don't have a bunker to hide in, knows the real meaning of *fire*. Bullets flying over your head are frightening, but the *crack-whump* sound of bullets pales in comparison with the abject fear you feel when you are in the open, exposed, and you hear a mortar being fired at you, and you have to wait while it flies toward you.

Al's prediction was close to being right. The mortar round hit almost directly on his expedient toilet. Actually it landed a short distance in front of him. Fortunately, Al was surrounded by thick jungle foliage, branches, tanglefoot, and vines. Unfortunately, however, the concussion from the exploding mortar round knocked him backward off the log, right into his own considerable pile of excrement.

Al was temporarily blinded, he couldn't hear, and he was in shock, but he instinctively rolled behind the log for protection while Viet Cong guns chattered. He pulled his trousers up and fastened them and realized that somehow he had grabbed his M-16 rifle before he had been blown into his shit, with which he was now covered.

The firefight was short-lived, as they usually were with Montagnards in greater numbers against ragtag VC, who decided that they wanted to leave and live to fight another day. Actually, Montagnards in lesser numbers would have still caused the same reaction in the Vietnamese Communists. They always did. Nobody wanted to fuck with the Yards, least of all the Vietnamese.

The Montagnard strikers set up a hasty perimeter and several followed the retreating VC to ensure against a second attack. Al and George Foreman ran from man to man to ensure that everyone knew what to do in case of another attack. Two patrols were quickly sent out, one as a blocking force and the other as a sweeping force, to try to catch the VC mortar crew. Al didn't really hope to catch them, but the try had to be made.

Finally, feeling that everyone was doing what was needed and was ready for whatever might happen, the two Americans met in the center of the hasty perimeter. As Al walked by, Montagnards giggled and quickly stepped to the side. George Foreman screwed up his face and held his nose.

"Muthah fuck, Top," he drawled. "You smell like shit! In fact, you are covered in shit! Git the fuck away from me! Damn!"

Al looked down at himself and saw that he was covered in his own feces.

Foreman grabbed his indigenous rucksack and ammo belt and harness and slung them over his sweat-soaked tiger shirt. He looked at the interpreter and said, "Tell everyone to saddle up and move out, Cowboy. Head for the nearest river."

While the interpreter relayed the orders and the strikers prepared to take off, Al just stared at Foreman, his jaw dropped open.

"What the fuck you doin,' George?"

"Top, you ain't comin' near me or anybody else till you take a fuckin' bath," George said emphatically.

Al couldn't argue with that, so he just went along with the operation, noticing that all the strikers stayed far away from him. An hour later, they made it to a river, and he took a long bath in his clothes.

Six months later, Al and his team members went back to Okinawa to First Group headquarters at Sukiran. They were ready to howl and let off some steam. The group gave them a formal dinner and dance at the NCO club. All the team members showed up in dinner jackets and had their wives in tow in nice evening dresses. The club manager told them that they could eat and drink as much as they wanted—the tab was taken care of. They were placed in a designated section in the main ballroom, and two waitresses were assigned to them. The club manager kept telling them to have a great time and dance, laugh, and eat all they wanted.

The group command sergeant major had cautioned all the men to be on their best behavior. He just wanted them to behave and not get rowdy.

Everything went well for several hours, until the drinks had sufficient time to accumulate. These men were Special Forces, and SFers were known to outdrink, outcuss, outfight, and gross out any other group of people in the world. These men had been in the boonies for over half a year. Some of them were still there, their bodies decomposing and mixing with the foreign soil. Here they were going to party.

Some SFers, in an attempt to gross out some Marines at a bar, had made a big joke. They would wait until a guy went to the rest room, then they would stir his beer with their penis while he was gone. This had been going on for some time, when some of the snake-eaters really got into their cups.

Charles Travers was always very polite and soft-spoken. But once he was on his way drinking, his timidity completely disappeared, and this was the case at the party. So it was no surprise to anyone when he loudly announced, "I gotta go to the latrine. Don't anyone fuck with my drink."

Everyone chuckled as he walked from the ballroom.

George Foreman captured everybody's attention with his loud guffaws, and all eyes turned to him: "Look, he wanted to make sure nobody fucks with his beer," he roared.

Everybody looked at the empty seat where Travers had been and saw an upper plate of dentures sitting in the bottom of the glass of beer. Around the room people held their sides with laughter. Well, everyone except the club manager. He wasn't laughing, and what happened next made him laugh even less.

There was a performer that night, a piano player from Paris, France, who played and sang songs for the crowd. The man's name was Pierre, and he was as good as you would imagine a Parisian piano player performing in Sukiran, Okinawa, would be. Thinking of his wife and well on the way to getting plastered, Al Fontes asked Pierre to play and sing "Autumn Leaves," which the singer did with reckless abandon.

While the crowd applauded, Al jumped to his feet and ran up to the piano player on the stage. "Pierre, you wonderful frog," he screamed, "that was abso-fucking-lutely beautiful!"

With that, Al grabbed the befuddled Pierre's head in both hands and stuck his tongue in the man's ear. Whereupon Al's wife looked for an exit door, while the drunken SFers roared with even more hilarity. At the same time, the club manager whisked his way quickly toward the laughing NCO and the totally unnerved performer. A wave of his hand brought two masters-at-arms, who unceremoniously escorted Al from the club.

At the door the manager said, "Sergeant Fontes, you are banned from this club for a period of one month."

The following day, Al found himself standing at attention in front of the group command sergeant major's desk.

The boss NCO said, "Al, you stepped on your dick with track shoes this time."

"Ah, Top," Al said.

He was interrupted, however, when the sergeant major said, "You are not to patronize any nightclub in this fucking country for the next thirty days. Understand?"

The command sergeant major just about fell over a few days later, when he and his wife entered a classy nightclub and were taken to their table by a tuxedoed Al Fontes. Al shook hands with the shocked senior NCO and said, "Top, you told me I couldn't patronize any fucking clubs, but you didn't say shit about working for one."

3

Snake-Eater

ONE MAN WHOM MANY included in their list of true snake-eaters was Jack E. "Happy Jack" Deckard, a major originally from Missouri and a full-blooded Cherokee. Jack always had a ready smile for everyone, but he was no man to be trifled with. Large and well muscled, Jack had piercing dark eyes that went right into a man's soul if that man was trying to fuck with him. I had heard many stories about Jack before I ever became good friends with him.

The first story I heard about this truly SF major was his ability to intimidate if he needed to. One day Jack was walking down a street in Da Nang, the story goes, accompanied by an old-time Special Forces sergeant major who had been friends with him years before, when Jack was a sergeant first class, or E-7.

Unhappy with his pay scale and responsibilities, Jack had opted for Infantry OCS at Fort Benning, Georgia, and was commissioned a second lieutenant. He had worked his way up to major and was the S-3, or operations officer, for FOB 4, or Forward Operating Base 4, of MAC-V/SOG in Da Nang with CCN.

Jack and the senior NCO were trying to hold a serious conversation while walking down the crowded street, but they were constantly interrupted by an old Vietnamese *papasan* trying to make a buck. The wrinkled old man was loaded down with numerous little bamboo birdcages with little yellow birds inside. Jack and the sergeant major presumed they were canaries, although knowing the marketing techniques of the Vietnamese, they figured the birds could be sparrows covered with bright yellow paint.

"Thieu-ta, Thieu-ta," the old man pleaded, calling Jack by his military rank. "Buy one bird, please? Five hundred P [piastres]? You buy, number one, you like same-same, Number-one."

Jack kept refusing and laughed to himself when he thought about the fact that the old man had called him *thieu-ta,* which means major. Although many so-called Vietnamese civilians were supposedly out of the war and unsophisticated peasants, he thought it was quite revealing that this old man could recognize and identify his military rank, even though Jack wasn't in uniform. In SOG they usually wore "sterilized" uniforms, with nobody outside knowing their ranks.

The old man kept bugging him, not taking no for an answer, so finally Jack stopped, his eyes shining like fire as they bored into the man's head. The man brightened, though, as Jack looked at the five birdcages and handed the old man twenty-five hundred dong (piastres).

He took the cages from the happy old man and then unceremoniously removed each bird from each cage and bit off its head, spitting it at the horrified old man's feet. He then replaced each bird's decapitated body into its cage and handed them all back to the old man, who could only stare, speechless.

Jack winked at the sergeant major, grinned at the Vietnamese *papasan,* and turned, walking down the street whistling.

Down the street, out of earshot, Jack chuckled. "Wonder if the VC are going to worry about the enemy they're fighting?" he whispered.

Laughing, the old NCO said, "Are you kidding? Those little fuckers are gonna shit themselves! It's people like you that make them think we're crazy as hell anyway!"

Jack looked at the man and grinned. "We're in Vietnam, aren't we?" he said.

The sergeant major said, "Good point. If we're here, we must be crazy as hell."

When I asked Jack about this story a few years later, he would not confirm or deny it. He just gave me a broad smile and started laughing.

Another famous story concerning Jack Deckard is one that went all over the country in the late sixties. That particular story is simple: Jack was giving a briefing in Da Nang, and a captain started arguing with him about a certain point. Happy Jack was not laughing. In fact, he punched the captain in the mouth so hard that the company-grade officer had to be medically evacuated to the United States.

The black-haired officer was much more noted, however, for his daring exploits in operations against the North Vietnamese and Viet Cong. Many didn't know who the man was, but many SFers heard stories of his daring with several recon teams in SOG. What many men didn't know at the time, though, was that the hero was Major "Happy Jack" Deckard.

Jack had become quite famous on one snatch mission. He had been in-country for some time, when a number of his teams were sent out from Da Nang on snatch missions. The S-2, or intelligence officer, had told Jack and the CO that he needed prisoners for some more current intelligence. A number of RTs were sent out into Laos to try to make a capture, but the teams had been coming back empty-handed for several weeks. It was essential to keep a steady flow of prisoners and not just *chieu hois,* as their information was not as reliable.

Chieu hois, technically called *hoi chans,* were NVA or VC soldiers who had raised their hands and walked up to allied troops yelling, *"Chieu hoi! Chieu hoi!"*

They then became a *hoi chan,* which had a different status as a surrendering prisoner of war. It was another one of those brilliant Vietnamization programs.

Many NVA soldiers would *chieu hoi* just so they could take a vacation. After giving up, they would be processed, sent to a *chieu hoi* reeducation center for two weeks, and simply walk away and return to their units with as much intelligence information as they could gather, feeling fully rested and well fed.

North Vietnamese counterintelligence agents were often sent out on missions to *chieu hoi* and then volunteer phony disinformation to the Americans or South Vietnamese interrogators.

At least with POWs, the American intel people knew that they could sometimes pry information out that was less likely to be false.

Frustrated with the inability of the RTs to capture any prisoners, Jack decided to set an example and lead a recon team out himself on a snatch mission. His team consisted of himself, a senior first lieutenant, and four very tough Montagnards, two from the Rade tribe, one from the Jarai, and one from the Bahnar.

MAC-V was badly in need of some current intelligence on troop movements in Laos, so three RTs from CCN were sent into Laos and told to pick up a prisoner along the Ho Chi Minh Trail, which ran parallel to the Laos-Vietnam border. The three teams launched out of

Special Forces border camps, and Jack's went about twenty kilometers inside the country, directly west from the dividing line between I Corps and II Corps areas in South Vietnam. The area was secured by the Second NVA Division, but numerous units swept through the jungle-covered mountains on the Ho Chi Minh Trail, which wound around through long valleys and steep canyons. In some places, giant lengths of bamboo were pulled across the trail and tied above it to make it impossible to see from the air.

In lieu of expensive electronic equipment, the NVA stationed trail-watchers at major trail crossings with a rifle. If an enemy unit came through the crossing, the trail-watcher fired a certain number of shots to indicate the size of the unit, then other shots to indicate the enemy unit's direction of travel. The life of the NVA or VC trail-watcher could be extremely dangerous; but on the other hand, it was also quite boring most of the time.

This was the case with the first prisoner that Jack's team snatched. Nguyen Van Minh (a fictional name) had grown up in Hue but moved to Vinh, North Vietnam, with his father, a sergeant with the Viet Minh, who had been badly wounded against the French at Dien Bien Phu. The father became a food and arms bearer, and the son was recruited to help him as soon as he was old enough.

When his father was killed by a B-52 strike outside Pleiku, Minh received a leg wound that was severe enough to preclude him from pushing his overloaded bicycle up and down the trail. He got the cushy job of being a trail-watcher, watching over a major infiltration trail running off the Ho Chi Minh Trail and intercepting Highway 14 in Vietnam between the Green Beret A-camps of Dak Pek and Kam Duk. U.S. intelligence in the area referred to Highway 14 as Alpha Road, and it was eventually used to transport Soviet tanks in country to overrun Kam Duk.

Minh carried a piece of paper with him everywhere that he had taken off the body of a young American from the Americal Division. The paper was the centerfold of a *Playboy* Playmate of the Month. Although that trail intersection was very important, it was not very busy during daylight hours, and nothing moved along either trail during the morning. So Minh took a break right after Poç time and pulled out the picture.

He stared at it and dreamed of touching the long, golden hair and the creamy white skin. Minh felt excitement, and the more he looked at the picture, the more excited he got. He soon laid his SKS rifle against a nearby tree and pulled his khaki trousers down around his ankles. He gripped his erection in his right hand and, moaning, pumped himself furiously. The Vietnamese man felt a cramp starting in his wounded leg, but he ignored it because of the ecstatic feelings in his loins and his overwhelming desire to be inside this mysterious white woman with the hair made from sunbeams.

The pressure and the sensations built until Minh felt as if he were ready to explode all over Laos. His breathing was coming out of his mouth in almost-sobs—when he felt something on his shoulder. Quickly he turned his head and stared into the barrel of an American-made CAR-15 assault rifle. Beyond that, he looked into the grinning face of Major Jack E. Deckard, teeth clamped around the butt of an unlit Cuban cigar. Beyond the American was another laughing American and four mean-looking Montagnards, also laughing.

The American spoke, but Minh didn't understand the words: "Hey, Ho Chi! Looks like yer dick just shriveled up. How come?"

At the American's signal with his rifle, Minh let go of himself, placed his hands atop his head, and stood up, trousers still around his ankles. He turned his eyes to see if he could grab for the SKS rifle, but it was gone. Glancing farther to the side, he saw one of the Montagnards holding the rifle straight out from his crotch and simulating masturbation on the barrel, while telling the other Montagnards a joke in tribal language that Minh couldn't understand. He could pretty much guess what the man said, however.

The other American jerked Minh's hand roughly behind his back, and a pair of handcuffs were slapped on his wrists. The Playmate was handed to the redhead, who in turn handed it to the Montagnards. They stared at it, eyes open wide, and giggled. Minh was gagged and blindfolded with American gauze bandages and pushed down the trail. He heard the dark-skinned American speaking into a little radio and a voice coming back.

Minh heard Vietnamese voices coming down the trail, and his heart leaped for joy. He felt himself being pushed into the jungle undergrowth—then something struck him on the back of the head. His head whirled, and the sounds of the jungle quickly faded.

Jack dropped Minh's body into the thick growth and felt his pulse to ensure he hadn't killed the prisoner with the rap on the head. The small patrol ducked down out of sight behind some elephant ears—thick, wide jungle leaves. An NVA patrol, riding bicycles, pedaled down the Ho Chi Minh Trail, cackling like a bunch of old hens. Jack saw a chance to take another prisoner. Each man in the bicycle patrol maintained a distance of about fifteen feet from the others. Jack also saw that the last man in the patrol was not talking or laughing like the others, so he was either standoffish or pouting.

Jack grinned, gave the other patrol members the shushing sign, and crouched next to the trail. The second-to-last man passed by him, and he tensed his muscles, ready to move. His right hand on the telescoped stock of his CAR-15, Jack waited, timed his move—then jammed his gun barrel through the front spokes of the last NVA soldier's bicycle.

Before the startled man could react, Major Deckard jumped up, wrapped a beefy arm around the man's neck, and clamped his palm over his mouth. Snatching him from midsomersault over the handlebars, he dragged him into the foliage. The red-haired American with Jack quickly jumped out on the trail, grabbed the bike, and pulled it out of sight into the jungle. The Bahnar quickly wiped away all tracks from the muddy black path.

The new prisoner was cuffed and gagged, like Minh, who was revived with water and slapped across his cheeks. The tiny patrol quickly took off to the east on the side trail that intersected Highway 14. Jack called in a spot report and requested immediate extraction. Within a half hour, the entire team was pulled out of the thick jungle on Mc-Guire rigs, folding T-seats on metal cables, suspended below two sterile Korean War–vintage helicopters piloted by very gutsy American-trained Vietnamese pilots.

In that one afternoon of bravado, Jack Deckard became a legend, as had so many Special Forces–types before him. But because of the top secrecy of MAC-V/SOG, many people heard the story but did not know who the man was. In fact, he took the team back out the next day and attempted another incredible deed.

The team crept softly up the Ho Chi Minh Trail through the thick, jungle-choked Laotian mountains due west of the area where I Corps and II Corps joined together.

They stopped for a break and crept into really thick

foliage on a small hillock overlooking the trail. The under-growth was so thick that they could see no more than five feet in any direction, so Jack let them light up cigarettes as they sat back to back, facing outward in a tiny protective circle.

The lieutenant whispered over his shoulder, "How the fuck we gonna catch him, sir?"

"Don't worry, son," Jack said. "We're going to look for targets of opportunity. In the meantime we'll pick up whatever intel we can on the area."

"What about a plan to capture someone, sir?" the lieutenant asked nervously. "What's our plan?"

Jack chuckled and whispered back, "Our plan, Lieutenant, is to walk around till we find someone, then figure out a plan to capture him. That's what the fuck I've been trying to get you guys to do for months now. It's as simple as that."

The lieutenant was stiff-lipped. "Yes, sir," he said.

Happy Jack finished his cigarette and crushed it out. He rolled the butt between his fingers and let the tobacco slide out and be carried off with the breeze. Then he rolled up the paper into a tiny ball and flipped it into the green wall around him.

All the men had been burning leeches off their calves, arms, and necks during the break and trying to ignore the mosquitoes buzzing constantly around their heads.

At a signal from Jack, the men silently moved down the hillside toward the unseen trail below. When they hit the trail, they headed north again, with Jack walking point. The lieutenant looked at Jack's broad back and wished he could be like him. He thought to himself, Man, that guy has a desk job and could be getting laid in Da Nang. He has to have balls made of solid brass. We won't be able to capture any more prisoners just patrolling around, though. We've been doing that for months.

A half hour later, Jack's hand suddenly went up, then down, to signal the patrol to stop and duck. The five other men silently did so and strained to see through the greenery all about them. The jungle was so thick, even on the Ho Chi Minh Trail, that the point man for an NVA squad-size patrol suddenly came into view. He spotted Jack and the patrol just as the men behind him walked right into his back.

The whole NVA patrol, totally shocked, turned around and took off the way they had come on the trail back to Hanoi. Jack's patrol took off in the opposite direction. All of them, that is, except "Happy Jack" Deckard, the crazy Cherokee with brass balls the size of elephants. Jack took off northward up the trail after the NVA patrol at a dead run. His men looked back and watched him, then turned after him, suddenly ashamed.

Within a minute, Jack caught up with the NVA patrol quickly scurrying up the trail to get the hell out of Dodge. Besides his CAR-15 rifle, Jack carried a sterile Colt .45 automatic on his right hip, which he now yanked out of his holster and brought crashing down on the head of the last man, formerly the point man. The others were hurrying so fast, they didn't even hear Jack, or the headlong fall of the last man on the trail. They just kept going north as fast as they could.

In the meantime, Jack lifted up the NVA soldier and hoisted his limp body over his own big right shoulder. He turned back south and headed for his own patrol. Jack hadn't gone more then twenty feet when he came face to face with the lieutenant, leading the men up the trail after him.

Jack laughed as he walked past the stunned young

officer, carrying the unconscious POW like a ten-pound sack of flour.

As he passed the lieutenant, Jack winked. "Learning to walk point and set an example sometimes, huh?" he whispered. "Good for you, son. Follow me."

The SOG patrol had trouble keeping up with the big major as he moved quickly down the path, his mind cataloguing clearings they passed that would serve as good extraction points.

An hour later, a big four-engine C-130 Hercules flew over the small hilltop where Jack and the patrol were taking their last break. The tailgate of the specially equipped aircraft was opened after the crew chief readied the payload for delivery.

The big bomb was on casters. It was a daisy-cutter. It looked like a giant dart with the ten-foot-long spike protruding from its nose.

The onboard computer locked onto the jungle-choked hilltop that Happy Jack had picked out for the LZ. He and his men had to get out quickly and didn't have time to clear the LZ or take a chance on a McGuire rig taking them out one or a few at a time.

The plane dropped its deadly load, and the giant spike took an attitude toward the hilltop. As the plane sped off into the distance, the bomb fell closer to the Laotian countryside. Five thousand pounds of deadly steel finally crashed through the triple-canopy jungle and headed toward the jungle floor. The spike stuck into the earth, stabilizing the bomb in an upright position, and buried itself all the way to the nose. Then the giant pyrotechnic exploded with a tremendous blast. Thousands of rounded steel triangles flew out from the bomb in every direction. Their deadly spinning, propelled by five thousand pounds of explosive energy, cut through every tree trunk, bush, branch, and clump of dirt in their way.

The dust and smoke settled quickly from the incredible heavy humidity, and in only minutes the hilltop was a barren flat area, capable of allowing as many helicopters as could fit to land on its flattened cap.

In the distance, Jack and his team heard the familiar *whop whop* sound of an old beat-up CH-34 chopper approaching, a ballsy Vietnamese pilot at the helm. They rushed toward the hilltop, clawing up the steep sides, yanking their legs through tanglefoot and vines.

Suddenly spotting movement at his feet, Jack froze. A green step-and-a-half lay at his feet. The bright-green bamboo viper's neurohemotoxic venom made its bite equivalent to that of a coral snake and a rattler at the same time. It was nicknamed a step-and-a-half since you could only take about a step and half before you died, once you were bitten.

Jack spat beyond the snake, and it turned toward the noise. He sidestepped quickly and charged up the hillside, soaked with sweat, but still carrying the limp body of his prisoner.

The chopper touched down as the team members emerged from the jungle; at the same time, gunfire erupted from almost three hundred and sixty degrees. They made their way to the helicopter while the door gunner and crew chief provided covering machine-gun fire. Jack, struggling since his heavy bundle was now starting to come to, was the last to reach the chopper's side, and the withering fire increased. He dropped the POW and held him up as a shield, while he backed to the chopper door. Jack heard gunfire over his left ear and looked up to see that the gold-toothed, grinning VN pilot was even providing cover fire for him with a .45 automatic.

Hands grabbed Jack, yanking him backward through the door, while other hands grabbed the prisoner and pulled him aboard, as well. The helicopter lifted off amidst a final hail of gunfire; some of the bullets bounced off the heavy added armor and others tore through the vulnerable parts of its steel hide. Jack heard a scream behind him as one AK round ripped through the shoulder of the door gunner.

The North Vietnamese suddenly stopped moaning and sat up open-eyed. Just as quickly, he gulped to the cocking of Jack's .45, which had immediately been stuck into his open mouth.

Happy Jack gave him a big toothy smile. "Welcome aboard, Ho Chi New-Jin," he said. "Don't bite down. We want to protect your teeth and gums so you can give us all kinds of information."

Wide-eyed, the little soldier tried to force a smile around the gun barrel. Jack winked and removed the gun barrel.

The man blurted out, "No biet."

Jack winked and tapped him between the running lights with the barrel of the gun. The prisoner slumped back onto his back, again unconscious. The major lit a cigarette and smiled at the lieutenant.

"Geneva Convention Rules," Jack said, chuckling.

The young officer gave the older officer a questioning look, and Jack grinned again. "Make sure the prisoner gets plenty of sleep," he explained.

He winked and took a long deep drag on the cigarette, thinking, Damn, this tastes good. Real good. "Happy Jack" Deckard and I became really close friends shortly after our turns in hell. I spent many nights at Jack's house, talking long into the night, and when his longtime wife, Ruth, and lovely daughters went to bed, I spoke to him of the stories

I heard about him. He never told me any stories about himself but would laugh his head off when I told him what I had heard about him from many others. In the early eighties, I gave up my heavy smoking, but Jack didn't. Sadly, he died a few years later of lung cancer; his last several months he was mentally back in the jungles of Laos, Vietnam, and North Vietnam. I bet that time, though, they let Jack win the war.

4

Civilization

THE THREE SHOTGUNS BLASTED again and again, and I ducked my head and hugged the ground as tightly as possible. The Bear Kodiak Magnum bow in my left hand was painted camouflage, as were my face, hands, and tiger suit. So was the aluminum arrow with the razor-sharp four-bladed broadhead on the end of it. The little depression I was lying on was only one or two feet lower than the rest of the ground, and I felt it was a miracle that the three men had neither spotted nor shot me yet. They blasted again, but I heard double-aught buckshot fly over me right before the *whump* of the gun blast itself.

Had they been observant, they might have seen the whites of my eyeballs as I stared at them. Then I thought I saw the short one on the left looking right at me. I squinted my eyes almost shut again, while he brought up his shotgun and pointed it toward me. I held my breath and tightened my diaphragm, waiting for the impact of the pellets. I tried to swallow but had cotton mouth, wondering if the pellets would penetrate my head or an artery. He fired, but the pellets again went harmlessly inches over my head. He still hadn't spotted me—he had merely been shooting this way.

When the three men turned, I wanted to scamper forward but forced myself to remain patient. I was glad that I was wearing a camouflage floppy hat instead of my green beret. This day, the beret would have stuck out like a sore thumb. As I watched them carefully, always ready to freeze in place, my left arm went forward and then my right. Next, my left leg went forward, and I pulled my body closer. I moved a few more feet, but they finally turned back in my direction while I was in midmove. I froze with my right leg an inch above the ground, pushed as far forward as I could reach. I held it there for five full minutes, and it started shaking from muscular tension. I tried to control the shaking, but it was too difficult. I prayed that they couldn't spot the convulsing, and so far they hadn't.

Finally, the men stopped shooting and turned away. I moved forward and straightened my shaking, cramped leg, flexing and unflexing it.

My eyes scoured the ground in front of me for the next twenty feet. Seeing no sticks or twigs in the depression, I decided to chance it while they reloaded their guns. I scurried forward to the giant oak tree. The shallow little gully ended about five feet from the tree, and I climbed up and darted behind the tree and hugged the backside of it as the three men turned around, shotguns loaded again.

The shots started coming again, blasting the bark on the mighty oak just two feet away from me, on the opposite side. I was now able to identify each gun by its sound, and I counted the shots from each. All three men had been shooting five shots per gun. I counted out fifteen and stepped out from behind the tree.

Normally, my teeth would be clamped down on the end of a Swisher Sweet cigarillo, and like Clint Eastwood in his spaghetti Westerns, I would take my time and light it, for dramatic effect, before speaking. For this day, however, I had wanted to make sure that I gave off no odor whatsoever. I had not smoked any cigarettes or cigars for twenty-four hours, I had soaked my body and my tiger suit in a baking-soda-and-water bath, and I had brushed my teeth three times with baking soda. After drying my clothes, I had left them overnight inside a plastic bag filled with pine needles. I was wearing brown-fringed, calf-high, soft-soled moccasins instead of my normal jungle boots, so I could sneak along and feel twigs and pebbles with my feet.

When I stepped out from behind the tree, the three men just about dropped their shotguns and cans of beer. I smiled broadly.

"Hiya, guys. How's it going?" I said cheerfully.

The three so-called North Carolina deer hunters had been drinking beer and blasting a target on the big oak tree with double-aught buckshot for the past hour out in the middle of Gun Swamp. In between, they had been eating bologna sandwiches and drinking their cans of booze while sitting on the tailgate of their pickup truck parked on the logging road. All of a sudden, some tall, slender guy in a camo hat, tiger suit, moccasins, and camouflage makeup and carrying a hunting bow and quiver full of arrows stepped out from behind the tree they had been shooting at. They all looked beyond me and the tree and could see no possible route I could have used to sneak up behind the tree.

One of them just kept shaking his head, while the biggest one asked, "Where the fuck did you come from, boy?"

I smiled. "Behind the tree," I replied.

He said, "Naw, before that?"

"Just been still-hunting for deer. Walking around the woods, enjoying the warmth and sunshine."

"You bein' a smartass?" the man said.

I beamed a smile through my green, brown, and black camo face paint. "Probably am," I replied. "I sometimes

do, but you can say just about anything with a smile on
your face, can't you?"

This threw him off momentarily, and he just stared at
me, scowling. Finally, he decided I had told him a joke. He
started laughing, and his buddies followed suit.

Getting a serious look on his face finally, he said,
"What if I would have shot you when you stepped out from
behind that tree?"

I grinned again and started toward the thick swamp
nearby. "You didn't," I stopped to say.

"But what if I did?" he asked.

I grinned again. "I would have killed you before you
got any of your guns raised."

He stared at his friends and then back at me. "Yeah,
how would you manage that?"

I smiled broadly again and winked. "How did I manage to get behind that tree without you guys seeing me or
shooting me?"

All three looked perplexed as I walked across their
front and disappeared into the thick foliage of the swamp.

I had done it again. I wasn't brave. Actually, what I
had done was quite stupid, maybe even mentally incompe-
tent, but then, I wasn't alone. One day, you are a Green
Beret captain. You are twenty-one, twenty-two years old,
and the highest-trained fighting men in the world are salut-
ing you and calling you "sir." You are in charge of other
men's lives in combat, and the decisions you make will
either make men heroes or get them killed. You are commanding the use of millions of dollars of equipment, and
the way you use it will either save or take away other people's lives.

The next day, almost literally, you come home, and
the adrenaline highs suddenly disappear. You walk down

the street and a few people ask for your autograph, but others sneer at you behind your back simply because you did what you strongly believed in. You watch the news and see people protesting and calling you a baby-killer and a rapist and a murderer.

The biggest problem, at first, was the end of the adrenaline highs. That's why so many Vietnam vets get, or got, into trouble with the law, booze, and drugs. Many times for the first few years, I had a simple attitude: Fuck it. That was what had happened with the drunken deer hunters. I am a conservationist, first of all, and have no respect for drinking slobs who are supposed to be hunting. I personally still believe that anyone who handles firearms and liquor at the same time should be jailed. I wanted to ridicule those men and make them look small without really causing a confrontation. I wanted to push it to the edge and see if I could keep from getting shot, while amazing someone.

There was, and is, a dangerous Incredible Hulk hidden away deep down inside of me. In a situation like that, one little SF voice deep inside says, "Terrorize them and destroy them!" It's a conditioned response, and it's in many of us and always will be. It has to stay hidden down there in the deepest wells of our psyches, locked away so it can never escape the way it did so often in that war. In the war, it was okay to let it out. Since then, there have been a few times when people pushed hard and tried to help it escape from its little cell deep inside my soul. They didn't know they were trying to let it escape, but I did. I even wanted it to escape myself, but I knew I couldn't. Nobody wants to ever see that happen again.

The winter of 1970 came and went. My A-camp at Dak Pek, A-242, was overrun by the Second NVA Division.

Spring came, and at the beginning of May my Incredible Hulk got one of his first tests. I had a loaded Army .45 automatic on my right hip and a loaded M-16 rifle in my right hand. I looked at the assembled Green Beret sergeants and lieutenants sitting in formation on the tarmac of Pope Air Force Base. Most of them were leaning back against their packs or parachutes and smoking cigarettes.

One nervous second lieutenant couldn't take it anymore. He leaned over and apparently asked the almost-napping master sergeant next to him to watch his weapon and gear. He jumped up, eyes open wide, and walked up to me. He saluted. I returned it, then offered him a Lucky.

"Sir," the young officer asked nervously, "I can't do this."

"Do what?" I said. "Board an airplane when we are ordered to? What's so hard about that?"

"Sir, that's not what I mean," he said, really shaken. "I mean, what if they really order us to go? Going to 'Nam to fight VC is one thing, but, sir, I cannot go to Kent State University and face American college kids holding a loaded weapon."

He paused. "I'm not even sure I agree with this war, Captain," he added.

I said, "Look, Lieutenant, I don't agree with this or any war where the President picks out the bombing targets, where the politicians run the war and not the generals, where we win all the battles but they won't let us win the war. I don't like fighting in a war where we didn't get the approval of the citizens first. I am also not going to shoot or order or allow anyone to shoot college kids. But you and I took an oath to serve this country as leaders of our best fighting men, and you and I are going to do that, Lieutenant, period."

"But, sir," he asked, "what if it gets really violent? What if we have to shoot?"

"We won't have to shoot," I said. "We probably won't even have to board this jet. If it gets violent, we might get some black eyes or bloody noses, but we aren't going to shoot any college kids."

"What if someone orders us to, sir?" he asked.

"No thinking officer follows or gives orders that are not in the best interests of the United States of America," I replied, then grinned. "Besides, don't fuck with SF if you can't take a joke."

He gave me a funny look, then broke into a grin and saluted. "Thank you, sir," he said.

I winked, and he went over to the sergeant and sat down against his parachute and rucksack. The old sergeant secretly winked at me, knowing, without hearing, that I had just been calming the fears and nerves of a young warrior before battle, an age-old requirement of military leaders.

We never did have to board the plane and fly to Ohio; the National Guard up there were supposedly taking care of the dissidents. It's a shame we didn't go. If we had, nobody would have died at Kent State. Special Forces wasn't like the rest of the Army; the men were "special," we were encouraged to think.

There were those who worked with us who were also very special.

5

Silent Heroes

THERE WAS A WEALTHY plantation owner in the Deep South who used to love to ride around his property in a carriage and admire all his holdings. Whenever he did this, he only felt safe if his lead slave, Luke, drove the mule team pulling the buckboard. Old Luke had been around for years and was expert with the whip and the words, the men and the mules.

It was a hot July afternoon when the two men rode down a long tree-covered lane between cottonfields. As the mules plodded along the twin-rutted wagon road, the plantation owner noticed a large hornet that landed on the rump of the off-lead mule.

"Luke," the man commanded, "let's see you kill that hornet without hitting the animal."

Without any noticeable effort, Luke swung the big black snake whip up overhead, lashed out, and killed the hornet without touching the mule's rump. The little insect's body disappeared with the crack of the whip.

The slave master grinned with satisfaction as they continued down the lane. It wasn't long before the plantation owner spotted another hornet on a leaf overhead, slightly off to the left. This challenge would require Luke to lash up and across, in front of both of them.

The rich white man said, "Luke, there's another hornet. Kill it without hurting the leaf."

As before, Luke did so with great ease, then continued driving the animals down the wooded glen.

A few minutes later, a hornet buzzed by the plantation owner's left ear and landed on a large hornets' nest that was hanging above the lane.

The man pointed. "Luke, there's another hornet. Kill that one without hitting the nest."

Luke didn't touch the whip and kept driving. The plantation owner grabbed a rein and commanded, "Stop the wagon!"

Quietly, Luke said, "Whoa," as he eased back on the reins.

The buckboard stopped with the hornets' nest almost directly overhead.

The slave master said, "You have never disobeyed an order in twenty-five years. Now, I said kill that hornet without hitting the nest, Luke. Do it now!"

Luke calmly replied, "No."

The plantation owner's face turned several shades of red, blue, and purple, then he finally blurted out, "No, you tell me no! What do you mean, no?"

Luke smiled and pointed at the hornets' nest. "I didn't mind killing the hornet on the mule's rump, or the one on the leaf. But not that one. See the nest he lit on? That's an organization."

The Montagnards of South Vietnam realized the strength they would have with an organization. In 1958 an almost-educated Rade Montagnard assembled several men whom he knew from the four biggest tribes. These tribes were the Bahnar, Jarai, Rade, and Kaho. He explained that the Vietnamese government would continue killing off all the Montagnards, stealing their lands, and ignoring their autonomy, as they had been doing ever since France

gave them autonomy on May 27, 1946. The only way the
Montagnards could resist, he said, would be to set aside
their tribal differences and customs and languages and or-
ganize. They should form a secret organization to fight the
Vietnamese, a secret resistance movement that would tran-
scend all tribal boundaries. Using the first two letters of
the names of the four major tribes, the secret movement
was called the BAJARAKA, and of course, members of the
U.S. Central Intelligence Agency encouraged and materi-
ally supported it. These good spies courted the Montagnards to fight for the government in Saigon. They promised the Yards that the United States would help them
regain their homeland and autonomy if they would fight
for the government of South Vietnam.

To please the CIA, Saigon organized an Office of Ethnic Minority and made a Rade Montagnard named Y
Bham Enuol the head of the paper tiger. He emerged as
the head of the BAJARAKA, which changed in 1961 to the
FULRO and FLHPM, as we saw in Chapter 2.

This organization, which I refer to as the FULRO,
had a tremendous effect on the operations of MAC-V/
SOG and the Fifth Special Forces Group, more than anybody knew. First of all, almost every Montagnard interpreter with SF and SOG was a cadre member, encouraged
and trained to get assistance, training, arms, equipment,
and guidance from the sympathetic Green Berets. Second,
most of the strikers, especially the better fighters, were
dedicated FULRO members, with one big goal: to get the
fine training from the SF people.

After Y Bham Enuol left the Office of Ethnic Minority to "bite the hand that was feeding him," the Vietnamese wanted his head on a plate very badly. They especially
wanted him after the Yards made a coup attempt in 1964
called the "Montagnard rebellion." Montagnards took

over five SF A-camps and held the American Green Berets under armed guard in their team houses, while they executed the Vietnamese in the camps. In some cases, they hanged the VN from camp flagpoles or dropped them in latrines and machine-gunned them to death. They also took over the Ban Me Thuot radio station and were going to transmit messages to all the tribes throughout the Highlands to join the revolt. The young lady who was going to make the broadcast was the niece of the man who founded the BAJARAKA, and her name was H'li. The only problem was that the Montagnards had nobody who knew how to run the radio station transmitter, because the Vietnamese kept all the Yards from receiving any education or vocational training.

H'li was a Rade from Ban Me Thuot. When she was a little girl, she had fallen in love with a young Jarai boy from the village of Cheo Reo who had moved to Ban Me Thuot so he could be one of the fortunate Montagnards to attend school, like H'li. The boy, Kok, fell in love with H'li, too, but unfortunately, they were both in grade school.

By the time they reached late teens, H'li and Kok were both totally dedicated to the Montagnard independence movement, and they put their love for each other on the back burner. Eager to help fight, Kok joined the FULRO fighting force and quickly moved up the ranks with his leadership, aggressiveness, and courage. He became legendary as a warrior, and before long, he was close in the ranks to Y Bham Enuol himself. FULRO headquarters was originally in Buon Ale A, just outside Ban Me Thuot, but Y Bham was forced to go into hiding in Cambodia because the Vietnamese wanted his head on that platter.

Y Bham sent Kok into Vietnam as the primary re-

cruiter and trainer for new FULRO members. He was to
go around to different areas in the Central Highlands, get
a job in each new area, and spend all his spare time training and recruiting new members from the tribes in that
particular area. It wasn't long before Kok, too, was being
sought near and far by the Vietnamese.

One of Kok's first jobs was for the First Brigade of the
Fourth Infantry Division when it was stationed in Pleiku,
before it went to Dak To. He worked as an interpreter and
got wounded on one of his first missions. Not far from the
triborder area, a MAC-V/SOG team from FOB 2 in Kontum were on their way back from extraction in Laos. They
took small-arms fire from the ground near the border.

Cobras from the Fourth were called in and hosed
down the NVA ground troops. Afterward, a company of
Fourth Division infantry combat assaulted into the area
and fought several quick firefights, capturing several NVA
prisoners. Kok was flown out to the area to interpret for
the S-2. On the way, however, they decided to fly into the
area and pick up the weapons left behind by the NVA
when they surrendered. The Cloverleaf troops had already
been extracted from the area where the firefight took place
and returned to the company's perimeter that had been set
up.

One of the slick Huey choppers on a BDA mission
low-leveled a swampy spot and thought he spotted three
AK-47s lying in the mud where an NVA position had been
cleared away in the elephant grass. Kok and the several
riflemen with him were going to drop down and pick up
the enemy rifles. When the chopper made its descent, however, a squad of NVA popped out of spiderholes in the
treeline and opened fire.

The Huey went skyward rapidly and banked sharply
away from the fire. Kok felt something hit the edge of his

finger, shattering the knuckle, and his head snapped back as a sharp pain crossed his lip and right nostril. He fell on his back, his head landing on the left thigh of a Fourth Division corporal.

The corporal looked at Kok and shouted, "Oh fuck, man! He got shot in the fucking face!"

Kok was shocked, and when he tried to shake his head to clear the cobwebs, he saw blood splatter on the Americans. It finally dawned on him that he had been shot. Two of the GIs grabbed him and tried to help him out. Kok put his hand up to his lip and nose and drew it away drenched with blood. His finger started burning, and he looked at it, seeing it was bent to the side. He figured out what had happened while the soldiers were wrapping him with American gauze bandages from their ammo belts: When the Huey had banked away from the NVA, a bullet struck the edge of his left index finger, breaking it, and passed through the edge of the joint, cut his lower lip, and actually lodged in his left nostril.

The soldiers laid Kok on his back and kept reassuring him that he was going to be fine. They told him he was on his way to the Seventy-first Evac Hospital in Pleiku and that they would make sure he got the best care possible. At that time, he had trouble understanding them, as he was thinking in Jarai.

In the hospital he was indeed treated like an American, and the soldiers even told him they would see that he got a Purple Heart, a medal given only to Americans for wounds received or death in battle. Their promise was well intended, anyway.

What Kok didn't know at the time was that Vietnamese military intelligence had found out he was wounded. He got official-looking papers that he was to fly to Ban Me

Thuot to meet with some U.S. Army brass and work as a high-level interpreter.

Kok was excited, since he had family and H'li near Ban Me Thuot. He hopped a flight to the Central Highlands population center but saw trouble as soon as he landed. QCs—the Vietnamese "white mice" military police —were everywhere, and they were after him. After missing his first flight, he had bummed a ride on a U.S. supply plane and offloaded before they could figure out where he was. Kok saw various white mice, however, closing in on him and speaking into radios shortly after he deplaned. He rushed through the crowd and tried in vain to find a way to escape. The faster he tried to get away, the faster the QCs encircled him. Kok headed toward the airport terminal and made it inside with numerous white mice on his heels. Once inside, he spotted even more closing in around him.

The young Montagnard finally broke into a run and tried every door he came to. The crowd inside the terminal was thick, and Kok was very grateful for that. He tried one door that led into a hallway and spotted some writing that indicated that it was an American office, but it was dark inside. Kok tried the main door, and it was unlocked. He rushed in and locked the door. Several QCs appeared in the hallway, and Kok scrambled on his knees across the darkened office. He heard them try the door, then heard angry voices. He clearly heard one, apparently in charge, tell someone to get a key for the door. Kok slid across the floor and worked his way over to a door on the far side of the office.

Kok saw that the inner office light was on, but apparently nobody was around. Having no choice anyway, he reached up, twisted the knob, opened the door, and darted in, quickly closing it behind him. Kok heard the outer office door being opened. He looked under the door and saw the light come on. Kok turned around and stared right into the muzzle of a .45 automatic behind the very stern face of an American Army major.

Kok heard Vietnamese voices mumbling in the outer office, and he spoke quickly: "Sir, my name is Kok Ksor, and the Vietnamese look for me because they want to torture me and kill me."

"Why?" the major asked.

"Have you heard of the FULRO, sir?" Kok said quickly.

"Yes, I have," the major replied. "Are you involved?"

"Yes, sir," Kok said firmly. "I will not stand here with my hands up when they come through that door. I will die fighting as a man."

The major looked sternly at Kok and listened to the voices in the outer office.

Outside, the second lieutenant in charge of the QCs assembled his men before the major's door and told them to go in and search. One white mouse put his hand on the knob and turned it. The cocking of several guns greeted the major in his office.

"What the fuck's going on!" the major yelled to the QCs.

The second lieutenant bowed apologetically. *"Xin loi, thieu-ta*—uh, Major. A dangerous criminal has escaped, and we think he come here. Number-ten, bad man. Killer. Kills everybody."

"Come in and tell me about him," the major said.

He walked back to his desk and sat down, while the lieutenant and two MPs walked around the room and looked all over, their eyes searching every nook and cranny. The QC lieutenant spent several minutes telling the major about the dangerous killer Kok Ksor. Finally he left.

The major rolled his chair back, and Kok crawled out from under the desk, totally drenched with sweat.

He stuck his hand out, and the two shook. "Thank you very much, sir. You saved my life," Kok said.

"That's all right," the American said. "I've heard, ever since I've been here, about how badly the Vietnamese treat the Montagnards. I'm going to leave and lock this office and the outer office. The lights will be out, and nobody will be here until morning. Good luck to you."

Kok got tears in his eyes and tried to speak but couldn't. They shook hands again and the American left, a big smile on his face. Kok sat down in the man's over-stuffed chair and looked out the window, shaking, and waited for the QCs to give up and leave to search else-where. In a few hours he would go out the window and make his way in the shadows to Buon Ale A; from there, he would escape into Cambodia to rejoin Y Bham Enuol and the other FULRO leadership.

Not too many months later, H'li, now eighteen years old, decided she could take it no more without her child-hood sweetheart and would go to FULRO headquarters to find him. She had no idea where FULRO headquarters was. She only knew that it was somewhere in Cambodia. So she only had to pinpoint a spot within 66,800 square miles —no big deal for a young Montagnard woman in love.

For several weeks she battled with her parents, who refused to allow her to leave. There was only a war going on, with NVA crawling all over South Vietnam and Cambodia, and H'li couldn't figure out why her parents didn't want her to take off alone and search for her man, her love, Kok.

H'li had two friends who also had lovers in Cambodia,

so the three made a pact, and one night under a full moon, the three ran away.

For days, they went from one sympathetic Montagnard guide to another. They crossed rivers and were almost spotted by North Vietnamese several times. They journeyed to the border of Cambodia and deep into the country, traveling a long time in a box atop an elephant. Finally, H'li was led to FULRO's secret headquarters deep in the jungle in Mondulkiri province, in the northeastern corner of Cambodia.

Kok was washing his clothes at a nearby stream when an excited Montagnard rushed over to him and said, "Kok, come quick! Your wife is here!"

Kok stood up with a queer look on his face. "I don't have a wife!" he said.

The excited man said, "I don't care! She is here! Your wife is here! Come quick!"

Kok followed, shaking his head. But he had the shock of his life when he walked in front of the headquarters building and saw H'li climbing down off an elephant. He was dumbfounded. He stammered. He stuttered.

Somehow, Kok finally got out, "H'li, why are you here?"

H'li smiled. "To be with my man."

He said, "You have no relatives here. Where will you stay?"

H'li replied, "With you. You are my man."

"Oh, my! Oh, no!" were some of Kok's longer, more intelligible sentences.

The next day, the couple got married.

Shortly thereafter, Kok had to leave and return to his recruiting and training duties in Vietnam. First, he went back to Pleiku and started working for the Pleiku C-team mobile strike force (Mike Force) as an interpreter.

Walking through downtown Pleiku one day, Kok was approached by a young Montagnard and warned that he had been spotted and that the Vietnamese were searching all over for him. Kok knew of a school principal who was sympathetic to the plight of the FULRO, so he made his way through various neighborhoods, across roofs, balconies, and yards, and slid into a window in the school.

Kok had a .380 automatic pistol tucked into the back of his waistband all the time, but he didn't have to use it.

The principal walked into his office and was shocked to find Kok seated behind his desk. The young Jarai war hero explained his plight to the educator. The old man excused himself and returned in a few minutes with a Polaroid camera and took Kok's picture.

While Kok waited, the man put together a complete set of phony identification papers, giving Kok the phony name of Siu Ton. Kok was grateful beyond words and left the school feeling a little bit safer, anyway.

Eventually, Kok had to leave Pleiku in the middle of the night because someone had tipped off the Vietnamese that he was a recruiter for the FULRO. By then, though, he had recruited some more Jarai, Bahnar, and several other tribal members.

In 1968, during the annual Tet celebration, Kok found himself in a situation that would affect him the rest of his life. The North Vietnamese and the National Liberation Front made a countrywide offensive in 1968 that became known in the States as the Tet Offensive. It was the turning point in the war.

Kok ended up in the fight of his life defending H'li's village and the in-country headquarters for FULRO, Buon

Ale A. During the several days that Buon Ale A was under siege, Kok went through many pitched battles. At one point he was in a foxhole with two other Montagnards who kept harassing him about being a devout Christian. He had become one as a young lad, listening intently to missionaries who came to his village regularly. He was also teased occasionally by other Dega who held to age-old Montagnard beliefs in good and evil spirits who came from the thick, black jungles.

Three different hand grenades were tossed into the foxhole, and they all had rubber bands wrapped around the flippers. Each time one landed, Kok said a quick thank-you prayer, removed the band, and threw the grenade back at the NVA. An NVA soldier fired a B-40 rocket at them, almost point-blank, but it hit before the lip of the foxhole while the three men ducked. After they left the foxhole, it was hit by a direct rocket or grenade and exploded.

In another foxhole an NVA soldier pointed a rifle right at Kok's face from the lip of the foxhole. The soldier's head exploded from a bullet that came from behind him. The impact flung his body forward, and it landed directly on top of Kok. Later, when the other people in the hole removed the man's body, Kok was completely drenched in blood, head to foot.

Shortly after that, while Kok was still lying in shock, he felt the barrel of a gun shoved against the back of his head. The NVA pushed Kok's face into the puddle of blood and mud in the bottom of the foxhole and tied his hands behind his back with U.S. Army commo wire. The sixteen other Montagnards captured with Kok were all marched to a hill in the center of the village and lined up. Kok saw a ditch behind them and got tears as he realized it held the bodies of numerous men, women, and children he had known who had been mowed down by a firing squad and left to roll on top of all the other bodies.

Kok could hear the screams of village women and girls being gang-raped by NVA soldiers, and he prayed a prayer of thanksgiving that H'li was not there.

Oddly enough, one of the two men who had shared the foxhole with him stood next to him while they were lined up for the firing squad. When Kok started saying the Lord's Prayer out loud, the man asked him mockingly if his Jesus would protect them now. Just then, an NVA officer ran out by the line of prisoners, held up his hand, and yelled, stopping the mass execution. He explained that they had decided they wanted some current intelligence and some slave labor, so they decided not to execute this group of prisoners. The man next to Kok became a Christian.

The group was led off west toward Cambodia, their necks tied together as they were force-marched in single file. Mile after mile they walked and finally came to an area where decaying corpses of dead Americans and Montagnards were tied up in trees. Most of them had been tortured. Some were decayed to the point of being mere skeletons with flesh covering the bones.

Kok couldn't help but believe that he would never see his beloved H'li again.

They were taken to an expedient POW compound in the middle of thick jungle northwest of Ban Me Thuot. At night their legs were locked in wooden stocks, and in the daytime they were made to work hard, growing mountain rice, potatoes, and other vegetables. Every day, they were fed one potato each. It got to the point where Kok's stomach hurt almost twenty-four hours per day. He just assumed that one day, they would all be executed like all the prisoners that were now tied and nailed to so many trees.

Incredibly, after several months, the seventeen prisoners were rounded up and brought as a group to the POW camp commander. Kok still bore fresh scars on his face and finger from the bullet and a scar on his arm from being wounded with the Pleiku Mike Force. The camp commander told them they were all free to go and gave them general directions to Ban Me Thuot.

Kok could not believe it. The whole group walked away from the camp, as simple as that. As soon as they rounded the first bend in the road, they took off at a dead run down the jungle trail. A mile later, they spread out into the jungle and gathered up roots, fruit, and grubs to eat.

The only reason they had been allowed to live that Kok could figure was that, as he learned, the NVA had tried to contact Y Bham Enuol on several occasions. The NVA wanted to convince him that the FULRO should stand aside and let them fight the war against the Americans and Vietnamese without their interference. The NVA emissaries stated that the Montagnards would get the Central Highlands back after North Vietnam won the war, as long as they didn't get involved. Y Bham didn't buy it, but Kok figured maybe the NVA wanted to send Y Bham a message by letting obvious FULRO people live. For Kok's part, he just wanted to see H'li and their first child.

Using the phony identity of Siu Ton, Kok got a job as a bartender at the L-19 Airport NCO club in Ban Me Thuot while training Rade and Jarai recruits for the FULRO. One day as he left the club, he stopped when he heard the sound of about twenty guns cocking. He was surrounded by Vietnamese white mice, all pointing rifles at him. A Vietnamese QC second lieutenant walked up to him. Kok smiled and stuck his hands in his pockets. He cocked the loaded .25 automatic that was in his right pocket and decided that the Vietnamese officer was going to go to hell while he went to heaven.

An approaching U.S. Air Force jeep caused all heads to turn, and an Army Special Forces captain pulled up in the jeep that was being driven by an airman. Kok couldn't figure this out, but he sure was thankful, because the captain cheerfully marched up to the Vietnamese lieutenant and literally put him on the spot, escorting Kok out of the clutches of the tiger's paws. Kok pleaded that he was Siu Ton, while the lieutenant swore that he was a dangerous criminal named Kok Ksor. The captain asked why the military would be after a criminal and essentially swept Kok into his jeep, stating that Kok had been hired as the interpreter for his A-team. As they drove away down the road, the captain explained to the astounded Montagnard that he had intervened because he knew what happened to Montagnards who were taken away by the Vietnamese QCs. Kok was overwhelmed, which helped endear him to Americans even more.

Kok had still another narrow escape, this one from Ban Me Thuot, where he was working as a radio operator for USAID. His boss's name was George Gaspard, and Kok liked him a lot. Late one afternoon, however, a Montagnard came to Kok and warned him that the Vietnamese had staked out his apartment and were going to get him. Kok went to George and asked for an emergency leave as his grandfather was dying. George told him he could go but said he should wait until the following day. Kok buried his head in his hands and pretended to cry his eyes out. Feeling very bad, Gaspard told Kok to call himself an aircraft and fly out on it right away. George was such a nice guy and good boss, Kok felt horrible tricking him like that, but he wanted to live.

In Nha Trang on another job, Kok was working at Pacific Architect and Engineering while secretly training new FULRO recruits with the Fifth Special Forces Group Mike Force. He shared an apartment with two Filipinos. One afternoon, when he was walking home after work, he stopped right before he turned the corner onto his street. He just happened to notice a QC jeep parked back in a driveway near his apartment. He carefully looked all around and spotted a number of hidden QCs staking out his apartment.

Kok quickly made his way to the Mike Force compound, and the Yards there smuggled him out past the white mice. As they drove by the apartment, Kok peeked out from under the canvas on the two-and-a-half-ton truck and saw a QC officer harshly interrogating his two roommates in front of the apartment building.

During yet another escape, Kok was halted in a taxi by a roadblock with a QC and an American MP. Each military cop took one side of the cab and went through the occupants' luggage. Kok was carrying a duffel bag with a .380 automatic hidden under a blanket near the bottom. If he were caught with the gun, he would be arrested as a Viet Cong. Kok really sweated it as the American cop dug lower and lower in his bag. A scant few inches from the gun, though, Kok's own words stopped him.

"Oh, come on, sir," he said. "I'm a college student."

The MP was pleased to hear the good English and stood up. "Damn, you speak good. You an interpreter?" he asked.

Kok enthusiastically said, "Yes, sir, I am."

The MP smiled and waved him on.

Then, while boarding a plane, Kok spotted a Vietnamese priest who had taught him in high school. So few Montagnards were able to get into high school that Kok stood out in the man's memory like a sore thumb. The priest had been apprised of Kok's status as a very wanted man by Saigon. He spotted Kok at the same time Kok spotted him, and the priest immediately made his way toward the QCs all over the airport. Kok hurried aboard the plane, shaken, and watched helplessly out the window, but the plane took off before the priest could get to the white mice. When Kok deplaned, he showed his papers with the phony name Siu Ton and wasn't even questioned. They were looking for a dangerous Jarai named Kok Ksor.

After Prince Norodom Sihanouk was deposed as the head of Cambodia, the North Vietnamese really started wreaking havoc around the countryside. Kok had to get his wife and babies away from FULRO headquarters in Mondulkiri province. H'li cried and begged him not to, but Kok's sense of duty made him find a way to get them to Phnom Penh.

Not long after H'li escaped and Kok promised her that somehow, someday, he would make it to Phnom Penh and find her, he found himself in another major attack surrounded by North Vietnamese. Kok was with another Montagnard named Y Tieng as thousands of NVA overran their position one night, and women were raped and people were executed inside their own perimeter. The two men held until they knew they were surrounded in the rear and both sides, then crawled over the lip of their foxhole and slithered forward into the jungle. The other FULRO warriors did the same thing, and a number of them rendezvoused after daybreak, several miles away.

The group traveled several days, searching left and right for food and getting hungrier by the minute. Finally, one man took a big risk and shot a water buffalo. The water buffalo is a beast of burden in Laos, Cambodia, and Vietnam and is not used for food. Alarmed by the possible consequences, the group leader, FULRO Major Kpa Doh, led the men in flight away from that area. They got away safely, but a number of the men said they wanted to go back after the water buffalo. Kpa Doh, Kok, and others argued and argued with the group, trying to warn them about the stupidity of their decision, but the men let their stomachs make the decision instead of their brains.

The following day, Kok and the other men were walking along a ridgeline overlooking a dirt road. They were still in Mondulkiri province in northeastern Cambodia. One of the rear guard gave a warning, and the small group took cover. On the road below marched a column of NVA soldiers with a group of prisoners—the men who had gone back for the water buffalo. Their necks were bound together by wire, and they walked single file down the road. A half hour after they passed, Kok's group heard gunfire coming from their direction. Later they found the men's bullet-riddled bodies along the side of the road.

A few days later, they came to a village in the jungle that looked very quiet in the early-morning sun. In fact, it looked too quiet. Kok was very suspicious and told Kpa Doh that it had to be a trap. The two got into an argument, and finally Kpa Doh insulted Kok's masculinity when he told him just to hide behind the others if he was afraid.

Furious, Kok said, "Fine! Fine! Don't listen to me! I'll go first and lead the way into the village, but I warn you, we will all be killed. It is a trap."

Kok stormed off toward the village, and his friend Y Tieng fell in beside him.

Kok whispered, "There are no dogs barking at us or anything. I know it's a trap. So if the NVA ambush us, start firing and run straight ahead. They won't expect that."

Minutes later, hidden North Vietnamese soldiers opened fire from every direction. They had been hidden in every hut, behind trees, a haystack, and every other con-

ceivable hiding place. Kok and Y Tieng opened fire and
ran straight ahead, while the others were mowed down
trying to retreat out of the jaws of the trap. That was what
the NVA had planned for and had positioned their shoot-
ers accordingly.

Kok and Y Tieng made it into the thick jungle around
the village and got away clean, but they never saw the
other fighters again. They never knew how many lived or
died. They continued south, heading in the general direction of Phnom Penh.

Food was still almost impossible to find, and the two
men tried to subsist on roots and berries that they found in
the jungle. But for some reason, even those were scarce in
the areas they journeyed through.

At one point, Kok and Y Tieng were walking along a
trail through the jungle when they heard voices speaking
Vietnamese. The area they were passing through was kind
of like a clearing, but a jungle clearing is unlike any other
kind. There weren't any trees, but there were numerous
bushes and grasses that reached head high. A patrol was
approaching, and the grasses could be seen as they moved
closer. Just then, a tremendous downpour started. Kok and
Y Tieng dropped down in place and crawled just off the
trail. A platoon of NVA walked by within arm's reach of
the two Montagnards. In fact, one soldier stepped a little
off the trail, and his foot came down on the back of Y
Tieng's hand. Kok's palm closed over his partner's mouth
before he could yell.

The same day, farther on, the two men came to a
wide, fast-moving river. Using bamboo, they made two little rafts and put Kok's M-16 on the front one, their clothes
on the back one, and their heads in between. They kicked
across the river and lay down exhausted on the far bank.

Kok and Y Tieng, close to starvation, had another

close call when they came upon a small hamlet in the jungle. They watched for signs of enemy activity but saw none. They were suspicious, however, and they had only Kok's M-16 for protection.

Kok suggested that he go into the village, while Y Tieng covered him from the safety of the jungle. If it was safe, he would signal Y Tieng in and they would barter somehow for some food. Y Tieng said Kok was a better shot, so he should stay behind and let him enter first, so they did. As Kok peered behind two large leaves called elephant ears, he was reminded of the day they entered the other village when so many of their number had been mowed down. The jungle was very thick, extremely thick, and came right up to the edge of the tiny hamlet. Like the previous village, this one was quiet, too quiet.

Y Tieng was nervous, but he entered the first row of thatch-roofed huts. He walked slowly and carefully, looking both left and right. The NVA had been invading and taking refuge in all these little villages, so it made sense that they would be in this one, but he and Kok were starving. Y Tieng couldn't remember their last meal. He passed the first two huts and all was well. Maybe this hamlet was too isolated and the North Vietnamese troops hadn't discovered it yet, he thought.

Y Tieng looked at the second hut to his left. Suddenly he heard the sound of guns cocking to his right. Two NVA soldiers emerged from the second hut and pointed an AK-47 and an SKS at his head. Y Tieng gulped.

Suddenly, Kok's voice came from between the next two huts, and all three men snapped their heads around. Kok stood ten feet from the jungle's edge between the huts. He grinned, aimed his M-16 at the two NVA, muttered a few farewell words in Vietnamese, and hosed them down. Y Tieng's knees almost failed him, but he ran quickly to Kok's side, and the two ran into the jungle. NVA poured out of many huts.

The jungle was too thick. "Wait-a-minute vines," roots, branches, and tanglefoot pulled at their legs, while elephant ears, branches, bamboo, and billions of leaves obscured their vision. They couldn't see more than five feet ahead. They pushed and struggled as they heard numerous shouts and angry voices. Bullets splattered into the undergrowth behind them, but the foliage was too thick for the little copper-jacketed messengers of death to penetrate.

Kok and Y Tieng bulled their way through and finally sprang free. They fell right into the clearing at the edge of the village and immediately saw numerous NVA taking aim at them. They spun around and dived back into the greenery, as shots clattered into the thick stuff all around them and over their heads. The two men ran as hard and as far as they could, still in the thickest jungle possible.

Vines still pulled at their weary legs and their anemic blood was ready to give out on them, but they kept on. Kok was two steps ahead. The two men sprang free of the thick foliage once again, only to fall flat on their faces a short distance from more NVA soldiers in another part of the hamlet's perimeter. More screams and shouts went up as the two warriors, wide-eyed, spun and dived back into the green morass, shots chasing them. Again they pushed themselves beyond endurance, beyond mortal capability.

This time, they went in a straight line away from the village. They continued south, avoiding any and all contact with indigenous villagers and wandering bands of North Vietnamese soldiers.

One afternoon, the two men stopped for a break and lay down against the trunk of a large tree. They had found hardly any nutritious food to sustain themselves for days.

They could barely stand, let alone continue walking. After resting awhile, Kok stood, but Y Tieng refused to.

"Come on!" Kok yelled. "Get up! Let's go! We must keep going!"

"No," the other replied. "Save yourself. I cannot go on, Kok. I will die here, but you keep going and save yourself."

"Get up, you lazy stupid coward!" Kok raged. "You must get up now! You are Dega! Do not be a coward!"

Y Tieng smiled weakly. "I know you try to make me angry, my friend, but I cannot go on. You must save yourself, Kok. Leave me."

Kok got so frustrated, he started to cry and fell on the ground next to Y Tieng, who started crying as well.

"Kok! Kok! The enemy! The enemy hit me!"

Kok heard Y Tieng's words, but they were coming out of a dark well. The voice kept getting clearer and clearer, and finally Kok's eyes snapped open. He jumped as he saw that it was morning. Y Tieng was yelling, hiding behind the large tree. Kok stared at his wide-eyed friend.

Y Tieng said, "Kok, come here quickly! The enemy hit me with something on my head!"

Kok looked around and finally up, and then he started laughing. He laughed even harder and dropped his M-16 on the ground, holding his sides, howling with laughter.

Kok pointed up into the tree. "There's your enemy, Y Tieng! There's your enemy."

Y Tieng looked up and saw a monkey in the tree, just as the little animal took another piece of fruit and threw it down at him. The tree that they had both passed out under was heavily laden with some kind of fruit that Kok was not familiar with. The fruit, about the size of grapefruit, tasted good and was sweet. The two men ate and ate. In fact, they decided to make camp and build their strength up for a day.

Several days later, they stopped at the sound of far-off booms. The sound was unmistakable: It was the sound of war, the sound of weapons being fired and rounds landing. So the two Montagnard resistance fighters headed toward the explosions.

Two hours later, Kok and Y Tieng were wearing loin-cloths. They were carrying their trousers on their backs, having converted them into packs and filled them with fruit. They walked into the headquarters of an American mechanized artillery unit, which was actively carrying on fire support for an infantry in a firefight several miles distant. The two Yards created quite a stir.

The Americans couldn't equip Y Tieng with a weapon, but Kok was able to keep his M-16. The unit was in the III Corps area of Vietnam, southwest of Ban Me Thuot. After several days of stuffing themselves on American Army chow, the two men were escorted by a platoon-sized patrol toward the nearby Cambodian border.

Another day's walk brought them to the headquarters of General Les Kosem of the Khmer National Army of Cambodia, but more important, he was the head of the Champa Front in the FULRO movement. Like the other FULRO cadre, Kok and Y Tieng were immediately given jobs in the Cambodian army, with Kok receiving a commission as a first lieutenant.

H'li was cleaning the little house she had gotten for herself and her young children. Suddenly, she felt a chill and turned toward the door. There stood her husband and childhood sweetheart, Kok, in a Cambodian army uniform.

When Phnom Penh finally fell to the Khmer Rouge, Kok was attending the Advanced Transportation Officers

Course at Fort Eustis, Virginia, but H'li and the children were still in the Cambodian capital. With the help of numerous Americans, they were granted political asylum and got out just as the capital was falling under constant bombardment and attacks. They made it safely back to America and rejoined Kok, and they carried on the fight from here.

6

May Bay Chook Chook

THE VIETNAMESE word for airplane is *may bay truc tuong* (pronounced "mai bai truc tongue"). A good indication of the simple innovativeness of the Montagnards is the words the Jeh—another Montagnard tribe—used to describe a helicopter. They called helicopters *may bay chook chook*. When I asked my Jeh friend Nhual how that name came about, he said it was because of the sound of the chopper blades as they beat the air. The primitive people had no word for aircraft, so they used the term *may bay* from the Vietnamese and added *chook chook* for the *chook, chook, chook, chook* beat of the whirring rotor blades. Some of the Jeh villages used a different term because they had a different interpretation of the sound of the choppers, calling them *may bay cup cup*.

Much has been said about those crazy and fearless fools and heroes who piloted the rotary-wing aircraft during the Vietnam War. Many in Special Forces, and more specifically in MAC-V/SOG, sneaked into very dangerous situations and accomplished incredible missions, but they would still be there if not for the ones who flew into the jaws of death to extract them from the many dangers in that bamboo-laced hell. This includes those who flew dust-off, the unarmed medical evacuation helicopters with the red cross on the side who went into hot LZs to yank out screaming young Americans with hot pieces of twisted metal in their bodies or burning up with fevers from malaria or other jungle demons. Much has been said of these men and their courage, but not much has been written.

During the war, members of MAC-V/SOG and Special Forces were supported by all types of choppers: CH-34s with VN pilots, CH-19 Sikorskys, TH-55 Hughes, OH-13 Bell, OH-58 Jet Ranger, Huey Cobras, Hueys of every type, Chinooks, Heavy-Hooks, LOHs (Light Observation Helicopters, pronounced "loaches"), and more. The choppers could only do so much in the way of maneuvering, but some special men who flew them, especially some incredible medevac pilots, made those machines a hell of a lot more than their designers ever planned on.

One of those men was Al Nichols, born in Greenwood, Florida, who had entered the Army in 1957 at the age of twenty. Like many snake-eaters before him, Al Nichols had a very unusual military career, especially the beginning. He joined the Army and decided to jump out of airplanes, spending most of his three-year enlistment with an artillery unit in the Eighty-second Airborne Division at Fort Bragg, North Carolina. After "getting busted," as young paratroopers with wild hairs up their ass usually do, he finished his hitch as an E-4 but entered a Special Forces reserve unit while he attended the University of Southern Florida. He made staff sergeant, or E-6, upon his graduation in December 1963.

By this time he had accumulated six years of service in the Army, including three years in the SF reserves, so he sent a letter asking the Army for a direct commission to second balloon. They were happy to oblige: They made him a second lieutenant in February '64 and assigned him to Fort Sam Houston in the Medical Service Corps. From there, he went to Fort Bragg, assigned to the Sixth Special Forces Group. His initial SF assignments probably set him up to become the balls-out dust-off pilot he would eventually become.

Little did he know, when he reported to his original SF assignment, that he would eventually end up with a Distinguished Flying Cross, a Silver Star, Legion of Merit, Bronze Star with oak leaf cluster, two Air Medals with V device for valor and two oak leaf clusters, thirty-three other Air Medals, two Army Commendation Awards with V device for valor, a Vietnamese Honor Metal, and the Combat Medical Badge. He accumulated more than eleven hundred combat assault hours of flying time, was shot down three times, went down twice from engine failure, and was hit by enemy fire nine times.

Al actually served his first tour in 1964 and 1965 in the Mekong Delta area with Delta Company, when he was assigned as an executive officer/civil affairs–psychological operations officer of a Special Forces A-team at Tinh Bien. Originally called A-331, it was later reorganized as A-423. Under the B-team at Chao Duc, A-423 was located along the Cambodian border almost due south of Phnom Penh. It was less than a half-hour chopper flight to the Gulf of Siam. The area was notorious for being infested with Viet Cong. They hid in the Seven Mountains region along the border, which was filled with caves and elaborate underground tunnel networks. Two years later, a giant cavern and cave entrance would be discovered where many VC would hide from Al and his cohorts.

Although Al had a primary MOS in the Medical Service Corps, he was given a secondary MOS like mine, 31542. It meant a Special Forces–qualified infantry officer. Like I used to say, it also meant "nonelectric pop-up target."

Like everybody else on the team, Al took company-size operations and smaller patrols out to interdict or search for Viet Cong moving around the area.

One day in early 1965, the district chief came to the camp and reported that the Viet Cong had built a road-block in the Seven Mountains region. They would stop passing villagers and supposedly tax them but actually steal their goods or money. The VC were, as usual, very brutal, and several women and girls had been raped in front of their families. In several cases the husbands and fathers had stated they just wanted to farm their land and not get in the middle between the Vietnamese and the government of Ngo Dinh Diem in Saigon.

The team commander, Captain Charles Mendoza, assigned Al Nichols, now a first lieutenant, two American SF sergeants, and eight Cambodian KKK mercenaries to take a patrol to Seven Mountains and investigate the report.

Most of the area around Al's camp was rice paddy, with small patches of light jungle here and there. The land got more mountainous as it went into Cambodia, and it was to the west, where the Seven Mountains region lay, that Al led his patrol.

Two Cambodians moved about fifty meters ahead of the patrol as a point unit, and one sergeant and one Cambodian stayed twenty meters behind the main body as a rear guard. The jungle was too thick for flankers.

Al hadn't been shot at yet. Now in a leadership position, he was wondering how he would fare when the bullets started flying and the "pucker factor" went into full effect. He steeled himself for what lay beyond the next bend in the trail—or the sniper that had him lined in his sights right now.

He thought back to his college days such a short time before. That time had been so carefree, but now something was happening to Al that was different, totally different.

He finally put his finger on it: He felt alive, much more so than ever before. His thinking was much clearer, and all his senses were alert, totally alert. He was frightened, but his fear made him more alert and would keep him alive. He knew it would sustain him. He knew it with a certain confidence that he just couldn't describe.

They moved closer to the area where the roadblock was set up. Al noticed that his breaths were coming more rapidly. He didn't know if it was anxiety, exertion, or a combination of both. They stopped for a break, and when Al looked back down the trail, he noticed how much they had been climbing. A break in the tops of the trees showed him mile upon mile of rice paddies stretching out below them in the distance. No wonder he was getting winded.

The heat and humidity in South Florida had sometimes been devastating, but South Vietnam was different; it was like being in hell with broken dehumidifiers. Like all the other soldiers, the first thing Al got rid of in Vietnam was his underwear. The jungle fatigues would get soaked but fortunately would dry out in short order. The only problem was, he would have to find a place with no humidity to allow them to dry out. Maybe somewhere on R and R.

The small patrol rested for ten minutes, smoking cigarettes, burning leeches off their calves and shins, or dabbing Army insect repellent on them and removing the giant bloodsuckers. Al drank a full canteen of water and swallowed two salt pills as well.

Many of the Americans would drink enough water but forget to take the salt pills to replenish what they lost in their perspiration. They would end up with cramps, dehydration, heat exhaustion, or worst of all, heat stroke.

"Saddle up," the young lieutenant said in a soft deep voice.

The patrol moved forward toward the area where the roadblocks had been pinpointed.

A tough, wiry Cambodian was now point man for the patrol, and Al called a halt and hand-signaled him back to the main body.

While the two watched for movement, the rest of the fighters huddled together in a group around Al. He pulled out an acetate-covered combat map with several grease-pencil marks on it. The young officer pointed to their present location and showed the very close proximity of the reported roadblock. Cautioning each man to be on his tiptoes, Al wished the patrol good luck and warned them to lock and load their weapons and keep their thumbs on the safety.

Steeling themselves for the bloody task ahead, they stood and started forward. Within seconds, Cowboy flattened as a burst of automatic-weapons fire snatched the green floppy hat from his head. The jungle was no longer still and silent except for the sweet tunes of tropical birds and the constant hum of mosquitoes. The gates of hell had been opened, and Satan roared with anger. Demons screamed and gnashed their teeth with the sound of several RPG machine guns and Soviet Kalashnikov AK-47 assault rifles. Al and the other men flattened on the ground and took a few seconds to catch their wits.

Al raised his head and saw blinking lights of fire coming out of the green-blackness of the jungle on both sides of an expedient log-and-bamboo roadblock. He sprinted across the road. A sniper put a bullet through the leg of his fatigues. He dived into the foliage and rolled up against one of his sergeants.

Al was out of breath and cotton-mouthed, but he managed to catch his breath long enough to say, "Sergeant, you take the men on this side of the road and work up that side to where that big branch is hanging over the road there. I'll have the other half of the team laying down a volume of fire for you. Then you spread your team on line and lay down covering fire for us, and we'll move ahead about fifteen meters. We'll keep trying fire-and-maneuver and see if we can dig those Commie bastards out of there."

"Fucking-A, Lieutenant. Just give me the signal when you're ready, and we'll get it done."

Al nodded, winked, and took off across the road again under a hail of withering fire. He reached the other sergeant and Cowboy, the interpreter, along with the rest of the patrol. Using hand signals primarily, he conveyed what he wanted and got them spread out on line. They started laying down a heavy volume of fire toward the enemy snipers and automatic-weapons positions.

Al knew the other sergeant was waiting for a signal, so he popped a hand-held flare up over the road. The other team took off, while Al's half tried to keep the Viet Cong's heads down. The other team made it to the point Al indicated and plopped down behind trees and underbrush, opening fire on line themselves, while Al's team leapfrogged forward.

They continued trying fire-and-maneuver, a common infantry tactic, but fifty meters from the enemy roadblock they got pinned down by heavy fire from the hidden fortified positions.

Al had been on the radio with spot reports to keep the "old man" at the camp apprised of the situation. Now, however, he had to ask for help. A chopper had been already dispatched to the A-camp and was well on its way there when Al's call came in.

The team sergeant and several Cambodes were on a UHIB helicopter within ten minutes of Al's call. The chop-

per also carried a fifty-caliber machine gun and an 81-milli-
meter mortar and ammunition. Al and his men, using the
same tactic, fire-and-maneuver, withdrew and cut a quick
landing zone for the incoming helicopter.

Less than a quarter of an hour later, Charlie ducked
into their tunnels because it had started raining mortar
rounds. The SFers poured round after round onto the VC
position, then sent two volunteers forward in rushes, trying
to draw fire. It worked. The VC couldn't resist the attack-
ing targets and opened fire on them.

As soon as they did so, the team sergeant opened up
himself with the fifty-caliber and tore the VC positions to
shreds in short order. Al left behind a three-man security
force for the fifty and eighty-one and assembled the rest of
the patrol on line. They attacked the roadblock and wiped
out several of the remaining VC, finding blood trails for
several more who fled into the jungle.

An LZ was cut to evacuate the few wounded that Al
had, and a body count and damage assessment was made.
Al was in the midst of calling in an after-action report
when he spotted something he had never expected. Three
of the Cambodian mercenaries walked up with the heads
of three dead Viet Cong stuck on the ends of six-foot bamboo shafts. They stuck the bamboo sticks into the ground
next to the road where the makeshift gate had been, the
faces toward the east and west approaches on the two-rut
roadway, a warning to VC coming from either direction. Al
noticed that one of the heads had the mouth twisted into a
hideous frown, and the other a weird smile. The young
officer was reminded of the theatrical masks of tragedy and
comedy.

"They do this as warning to VC, *Trung-uy*," Cowboy
said enthusiastically. "VC see heads where gate was.
Maybe think tax villagers number-ten idea."

Al grinned. "At least they'll figure these guys were better off when they were ahead."

He heard loud laughter from the SF NCOs seated behind him, and Al Nichols knew that he had come through his first battle in good shape. The big lieutenant felt proud.

Two Hueys came in to pick up the patrol and its equipment. Al stared at the big birds as they approached. A big smile spread across his face as he watched their rapid approach and the speed with which they came to a stop and hovered before touching down.

Al was fascinated as the Huey chopper that picked him up cranked up and then soared into the sky, banking toward the north. He watched the jungles and paddies whiz below him out the left side of the rotary craft. He thought about flying one of these giant eggbeater-type crafts himself.

He imagined himself at the controls of the big machine and wondered what it would be like to be in command of such a powerful metal beast. He watched the Alpha Charlie, the aircraft commander, manipulate the tiller and controls of the big helicopter. He looked around at the crew chief and the door gunner, both seated behind swing-mounted M-60 machine guns, ready to spew 7.62-millimeter bullets out into the rice paddies passing below them. He looked at "Peter Pilot," the number-two man in the cockpit, as he worked some kind of button and talked to the Alpha Charlie over the helmet intercom.

Al listened to the powerful turbine spin the rotor blades around at the speed of hummingbird wings. He grinned to himself while he thought about the absolute freedom he would feel in command of such a machine, ripping the air with its big beating blades, as the chopped-up, used air piled up behind him like an invisible pile of dirt behind a burrowing badger.

As he passed above one rice paddy, connected to several more by small dikes, a patrol of local Viet Cong looked up from their hiding places inside spiderholes along the dike. As high up as they were in the chopper, Al could see the shine on two faces and was able to distinguish the other spiderholes as well. Suddenly, the door gunner opened up with his M-60 machine gun, every fifth round a tracer, as it spat flames down to the ground. Heads disappeared back into the dark holes, and camouflage lids closed over the spiderholes.

The Huey made a quick turn and fired a Willy Peter—white phosphorous—marking rocket into the dike, right in the middle of the spiderholes. A large plume of white smoke billowed up into the blue sky. The chopper headed home while the crew chief kept looking back at the ambush site.

He noticed Al watching and yelled over the rotor noise, "There's a FAC in the air, Lieutenant! He'll be here in less'n three minutes, and he's got some fast-movers on the way! They'll drop some eggs on those Noogens down there and blow their balls to hell and back!"

Al grinned and nodded, while the crew chief chuckled at whatever joke he figured he had just told.

In Vietnam the family name is said first, and the name *Nguyen* is ten times more common than *Smith* is in America. So, many Americans called Viets "Noogens."

Al was amazed at how easy it was to see the Viet Cong hiding in the tiny little holes in the ground. When he was looking up at choppers from the ground, he could never make out any details or see the occupants in the aircraft. But looking down at the ground now, he couldn't believe how easy it was to spot some of the smallest details.

He recalled parachute jumps he had made after dark and was amazed as he remembered how bright and light everything on the ground seemed to be from up in the night sky. On the ground everything could be black as night, but Al couldn't remember a night jump where he had not been able to see everything on the ground as if it were only dusk.

He leaned toward the door and hollered at the crew chief, "You know, these birds are one of the most important parts of this war!"

He really didn't want to express that thought to the buck sergeant—he was really directing the remarks to himself. It was a thought that just suddenly reached out and grabbed him.

Al thought back to the time he got to pilot the C7A Caribou. The pilot of the twin-engine plane was named Captain Stack and had said he was related to the actor Robert Stack. He had let Al, then a second lieutenant, come into the cockpit and fly the plane for a short distance, but that had been enough to make Al Nichols fall in love with flight.

On one other occasion, Captain Stack picked the young lieutenant up in a seventeen-seat Otter, a twin-engine plane. Some VC had been spotted, and the handsome young captain told Al to grab his M-16 and an M-79 grenade launcher.

Twenty minutes later, the pilot was flying over an area covered with paddies and dikes, and they spotted a squad-sized patrol of VC running along the dikes. The VC immediately started firing at the aircraft. Al leaned way out the door and fired the M-79 at the patrol as it took cover behind dikes, running when the plane passed overhead. Stack fired with one hand out his door, while Al leaned out, alternating between his M-16 and the deadly little M-79 grenade launcher.

It was one of the first adventures in the sky that had really started Al thinking about flying, but now getting close to his A-camp, he was seriously and consciously thinking about flying.

After a long shower at the team site and on his second bottle of San Miguel Filipino booze, Al leaned over to the team operations sergeant. "Top, I made a decision today. As soon as this tour is over, I'm going to go to flight school and become a chopper pilot."

The team sergeant took a swallow of Bier LaRue, a French beer popular in Vietnam, and said, "Lieutenant, why in the fuck you want to do something like that? You fly around up there in the blue sky, and the little cocksuckers take potshots at ya all the time. If yer on the fuckin' ground, ya can hide behind trees, in foxholes, or whatever. Just makes no sense to me, sir."

Al smiled and softly replied, "Top, it's just something I've got to do." Looking skyward, he went on. "I just know I belong up there, not down here."

The SF master sergeant grinned, winked, and toasted the large officer with his beer bottle. "Why, sir, whatever floats yer fuckin' boat. Just do me a favor. I like ya, Lieutenant, so whatever ya do, fly gunships, okay? They got tons of armor and tons of armament so ya can at least shoot yer way out of most shit. Don't fly no slicks."

Al chuckled and said calmly, "Well, actually, Top, I sort of figured on flying dust-offs."

The team sergeant spat his beer out and stared at the young man. "Lieutenant, no disrespect, but yer fuckin' crazy! I think ya got yer fuckin' brain fried since ya been over here, sir. Why in the fuck would ya want to fly a fuckin' chopper with no armament, no protection, and on top of all that, a big fuckin' red cross on the side of it, so's old Victor Charlie's got a bull's-eye to aim at easier? Now, why in the fuck would ya wanna do that, sir?"

Al winked and said, " 'Cause I'm SF, Top, and somebody's got to go in when it's hot and save the lives of our boys."

That caught the old Special Forces NCO in midstride, and he didn't know how to respond. He straightened up and looked at the young officer with renewed respect in his eyes. In dress greens, this man had tossed salad that climbed almost all the way up to his left shoulder. He had proved his courage many times over in the Third Infantry Division in the Korean War, some more on top secret FTXs in Korea with First Group out of Okie, spilled blood in South America with the Eighth Group, fought with the Mnongs in Laos, and displayed his bravery numerous times during two and a half tours already in Vietnam, and the war was just getting cranked up. If he understood nothing else, this man was a warrior and a hero, and he understood courage and a sense of duty. He would question the young lieutenant no more. The young officer was SF and had firmly implanted that in the NCO's mind.

In fact, nobody would have believed it, but the grizzled old noncom prayed silently that night for the officer and asked for him to be protected and to save many lives. For what lay ahead of Al Nichols, he would need more than one person's prayers. He would need those of many.

Fort Walters at Mineral Wells, Texas, had been hot, damned hot, but primary was over and behind him. Now that Al Nichols was in Advanced Flight School at Fort Rucker, Alabama, the heat and humidity reminded him of Vietnam. It was blistering hot, and the humidity seemed to drip off the clouds, branches, and leaves. It even seemed to weigh down words as soon as they were uttered and make them fall to the ground.

In one training flight his instructor had told him to go into a hover at about a hundred feet up. The grinning man had shut down the engine, and Al had had to stabilize the craft, letting it autorotate. Rotors and choppers are built in such a way that, when the helicopter falls from a hundred feet up or higher, the air resistance spinning the rotors actually creates enough lift that the helicopter can, if handled properly, autorotate safely to the ground. Al pulled back on the collective, waited until the back part of the skids touched the ground, and shoved it forward. The helicopter hit the ground and slid about eight feet forward. There was a slight jolt as it hit, but it was not the impact that Al had braced for.

The instructor gave him a wink and hopped out of the chopper. Al couldn't let go of the collective. He just stared out the front window at the horizon. After a few seconds he snapped out of it and looked down at his right hand. It had a death grip on the collective. Finally the young officer let go. After that, while unbuckling his safety harness, he noticed that his jungle fatigues were totally soaked with perspiration. Al chuckled at himself and hopped out of the Huey, whistling as he walked over and joined the instructor.

Al wondered if he would have to autorotate with no engine when he returned to Vietnam as a medevac pilot. He thought about getting shot down and wondered if it would happen to him. How would he fare if a bird was shot out from under him? Little did he know that he would be shot down three times and go down twice more with engine failure. Little did he know that aircraft he flew would be hit by enemy fire on nine separate occasions.

* * *

The air base where Al was stationed was at Soc Trang, between the peninsula and Can Tho, farther south and east than his original A-camp location. In support of Navy SEALs, he had flown a UHIB Stingray gunship, a chopper that was armed, among other things, with twin thirty-caliber machine guns on pedestal mounts. He had also flown some slicks, but he was accomplishing his goal, which was to fly medevac. His radio call sign was "Dust-off 85."

One day, he was sent out after a Ninth Infantry Division LRRP, or long range reconnaissance patrol, that was in deep shit. They had gotten into heavy fighting with a whole bunch of Viet Cong in black pajamas. The PJ-wearers, however, apparently weren't ready for naps. They were carrying instruments unsuited for sleeptime except to create nightmares. Al was in the lounge trying to have a drink and relax after doing too many missions to go in and take out wounded to evac hospitals. He was wiped out, but still he had to go. Even if he didn't have to go, he still had to go.

It was only a matter of minutes before Al and his dust-off crew were airborne. They warmed up the turbines, and the crew chief checked out everything on the list Al insisted be checked out before each flight. The engine revved up while Al pulled back on the collective and let her rip. Minutes later, they sailed through thick, wet blue air several thousand feet over the Plain of Reeds.

"Ohio-Hammer, this is Dust-off Eight-Five. Throw me a smoke. Over," Al said on the air-to-ground radio.

Of the eleven-man LRRP team on the ground, ten were wounded. Al wanted to get them out but quick. He saw that they were surrounded by VC, and those little guys weren't very particular about abiding by the rules of the Geneva Convention. The aircraft commander was WO-2

Robbie Robinson, and Al was glad. The man created a loud clanging noise whenever he walked.

Al saw lightning-bug winks coming from the muzzles of the VC rifles down below, and he would sometimes hear the cracking noise as the bullets whizzed close by his moving perch. The ground below was a series of terraced square-shaped mud puddles, covered by a thickening veil of smoke from bullets and explosions. Al saw one of the people on the ground toss out a grenade and red smoke start pouring out from it.

The young pilot said, "I see red. Over."

A voice, out of breath and frightened, came back, "That's Eight-Five. Get my men out of here. Over."

A pair of bullets tore through the bottom of the aircraft's fuselage as they started down to the expedient LZ. Al looked at his fuel gauge—it registered 850 pounds of fuel left. He continued his descent toward the landing zone as more bullets tore through the aircraft. He turned and looked into the grinning face of Robbie Robinson, who gave him a reassuring smile.

Al grabbed the radio mike and called, "Mayday. Mayday. This is Dust-off Eight-Five, and we have been hit and are going into hot LZ, already reported. Need cover and help to get out alive. Mayday. Out."

There was a small, L-shaped treeline of jungle surrounding the paddy where the LRRP team had made its stand. Viet Cong were everywhere, and they were pouring numerous bullets at the medevac aircraft. Al heard bullets tear into it and scream through both sides as the skids touched down. The whole scene was pandemonium. The crew chief screamed as he fell face forward out of the medevac with bullets in both thighs. He hit the ground and rolled several times, covering himself inadvertently with a thick coating of mud and blood.

Robbie yelled, "Cover me, Al!" and jumped out of the chopper, running to the crew chief and pulling him back to the chopper.

The grunts were loading other wounded onto the medevac while Al reached over, grabbed his M-16, and started firing cover fire out his window. As soon as Robbie got the crew chief loaded, he turned and saw another man trying to make it to the chopper.

The man was crawling on hands and knees. Even from his seat, Al could tell the man was bleeding from two sucking chest wounds. Blood dripped continuously from his mouth.

Al continued to fire with one hand and maintain the chopper with the other. The fuel gauge was now registering only 250 pounds of fuel left, although it had just read 850.

The second lieutenant helping carry and load wounded onto the chopper had a large piece of his fatigue jacket shot away, and the bare bone of one of his ribs was showing. The young man ignored it, as he continued to care for his men.

A spec four who also was helping load wounded looked at Al, his eyes wide with fear.

He yelled, "Sir, I'm the only one who's not wounded! You aren't going to leave me, are you?"

Al grinned warmly despite the situation. "Fuck no, soldier. Don't you worry yourself! We all go out together, or we don't go at all."

The spec four smiled, and tears appeared in his eyes as he turned and grabbed a buddy shot through the shins.

Al glimpsed black-pajama-clad figures dodging and weaving among the trees, trying to move toward the aircraft. The last wounded man was squeezed onto the dust-off, and Al pulled back on the collective. The chopper strained and the rotors whirred—but it was stuck in the mud.

There was a loud crash, and Al jumped, suddenly realizing that a bullet just smashed into his radio. He kept pulling back on the collective, and finally the big beast broke free of the mud and jumped into the blue sky, a withering hail of small-arms fire accompanying its ascent.

None of the gauges worked, and the radio was totally dead. The power was not even close to what it was on the trip there. Al smashed into the top of a tree, and the bottom of the cockpit bubble shattered, showering VC below with tiny pieces of Plexiglas. The chopper banked sharply to the left and limped along as quickly as Al could coax it. In minutes he was able to straighten it out in a level attitude.

The VC were behind them, and Al aimed the big bird at a long dirt road to his left front. It ran through a number of villages to and through Soc Trang. He banked right as he reached the road and traveled directly over it.

The medic screamed, and Al turned his head, as did Robbie, who was helping the medic attend to the wounded. Beyond the medic, Al saw that a wounded soldier had fallen out the door and was half-sitting, half-lying on the starboard skid.

"Don't let go, buddy!" Al yelled. "We're going to save you!"

Al aimed the wounded aircraft at the dirt road, and it started dropping quickly toward the ground. A hamlet lay ahead within sight. The bird dropped and skimmed along the roadway. It dropped even more and was now only inches above the surface. Al tried to pull back on the collective, but the chopper just had too many wounds to pay much attention to what the boss wanted. The back of the skids hit the road surface, and the chopper started sliding along the ground. It slid for twenty feet and came to a sudden stop. Al looked back. The medic had reached out and held the wounded man in place on the skid. He was okay.

Al turned and saw a man already heading toward him from the village. The man wasn't so far away that Al couldn't make out the AK-47 slung across the black-pajama-clad man. The villager/VC was riding a Honda motorcycle. Al grabbed his M-16 and slammed a new magazine in, jacking a round into the chamber. He leaned out the window, flipped the selector switch on auto, and fired a ten-round burst just a few feet over the approaching man's head.

Al and the others watching chuckled as the Honda slid sideways. The man quickly swapped ends and took off back to the village.

Al looked at one of the wounded soldiers. "That'll do more good than shooting him. He'll spread the word to all the other bandits in the hamlet."

The young soldier nodded and laughed.

The Ninth Division lieutenant, his exposed rib now bandaged, ran up to Al's door. "Hey, man, just got word on our Prick-25," he said. "A company of ARVN infantry's on its way in choppers. ETA is two minutes, and there's a slick and dust-off behind them coming for us."

"Outstanding!" Al said.

He and the lieutenant shook hands and smiled broadly at each other.

The lieutenant said, "You know—if it wasn't for you guys and your brass balls, we wouldn't—well—we—"

Al interrupted, "You know, Lieutenant, you ought to check on your men."

The lieutenant said, "Fuck, what I'm trying to say—"

Al said, "I know what you're trying to say. Forget it:"

The small group, some wrapped in white and red bloody bandages, formed a ragtag perimeter around the downed helicopter and waited. Within minutes, Al's heart lifted as he heard the far-off *beat beat* sound of approaching Hueys. A second later, some of the soldiers heard the sound, and Robbie Robinson spotted them coming, dots on the horizon.

Al and Robbie threw out smoke grenades on both sides of the road. Even the faces racked with pain had big smiles on them as ten UHIB slicks flew in, in formation, and landed all around the downed medevac. After the company came in and surrounded the group, another slick and a dust-off flew in and landed.

Al thought of his bottle of San Miguel as the sun shimmered off the surface of the terraced rice paddies down below. He wasn't thinking about the Silver Star that would come out of this day's work, or what lay ahead tomorrow. He thought about an ice-cold bottle of Filipino beer.

Al looked around at the wounded soldiers and wondered how many more he would be hauling out of hot LZs. He wondered if there was an SKS or AK-47 out there somewhere with a bullet in it meant for him. Al chuckled and wondered how many bottles of San Miguel he would be able to put away before midnight. The next day, he would be up in the skies again, piloting one of those flying targets around.

7

Playing War

I SAT IN THE door of the Huey as it banked sharply to the left, and leaned back, my hands pressed hard against the textured steel floor of the craft. I looked at the sergeants seated on both sides of me, and we gave each other those "I'm not scared, but you can't shove a pin up my ass" looks. I looked down at the tops of the trees several thousand feet below us and felt the hot moist air blasting me in the face. The trees suddenly turned into sand, and I saw yellow smoke swirling out of a grenade. I looked up at the red and green light behind the aircraft commander's seat. The light switched from red to green.

A hand tapped my back, and a voice behind me yelled, "Go!"

I yelled, "Airborne!" as I shoved down hard with both hands and kicked my feet out beyond the skids of the chopper.

I fell and fell and started counting to six by thousands, but at five I felt the parabellum canopy of my MC-1 chute open up. I looked up and checked my risers and suspension lines and the canopy above me. Everything was fine, but one of the two sergeants next to me looked as if he were going over the trees. Like me, he pulled the pins on his shoulders and started pulling the front and back of each riser. We tried to steer ourselves as close as possible to the turn-in point down below.

St. Mere Eglise Drop Zone on Bragg was the worst DZ on the post, so naturally it was used by SF. These "Hollywood jumps" on Saturday morning were the idea of JFK CG Edward Flanagan and were a lot of fun. There was a set of bleachers on the DZ, and the wives and families of the troopers would come out and take pictures or watch as sortie after sortie went up a few grand and spewed its olive-green bowels out into the air. Each man tried to maneuver the closest to the deuce-and-a-half and trailer that were the turn-in point for our reserves and rolled-up chutes.

On my stick, the sergeant to my left landed in the top of a sixty-foot pine, fell out, and broke his hip. The one on my right steered down and broke a wooden spine on the canvas top of the deuce-and-a-half.

The jumps, rappelling, and war games provided some adrenaline highs, but they weren't the war, and I was a warrior.

While Al Nichols was flying wounded out of the paddies and light jungle in the Mekong Delta, I had been in the highest, roughest mountains in 'Nam, up north, trying my best to keep from becoming one of the wounded myself. Now my mind kept going back, and so did my desire.

Colonel Arntz had been group commander of the Third Group and had pinned my captain's bars on me. I felt sorry for him because he had inherited a problem from previous group COs. The men who were billeted in the Third Group barracks just simply would not clean the barracks enough to pass any kind of inspection. They would get gigs like crazy on every inspection and would be restricted to the base or even Smoke Bomb Hill, but the barracks just would never get cleaned.

This continued until the Third Group got a new CO:

Colonel Robert C. Kingston. The first day I saw him, I correctly guessed that he would be a two-star general in a few years, commanding all of Special Forces as CG of JFK Special Warfare Center, or as it was called in those days to soften the sound of it, the JFK Center for Military Assistance. I knew then that he would become a four-star general before retiring. Nobody who was there when Bob Kingston took over could have doubted that this man was the CO, the "old man."

I sat at the shiny multicolored conference table in the Third Group conference room. The table was shaped and painted just like the flash on our beret. It was Colonel Kingston's first official day as Third Herd commander.

He looked at good-looking Major Lopez, the Delta Company CO, who was also in charge of the barracks. "Major Lopez," he said, "this morning when I conducted the inspection of the barracks buildings, I found them to be in disrepair and totally filthy. As soon as this meeting is over, you will call a formation of all Third Group soldiers who live in the barracks. Instruct them that they are to run in and get their field gear, including pup tents. Each man is to pitch his tent on the lawn of the barracks in a uniform formation and will live in the tent until the barracks pass my inspection. They will let you know when they are ready for me to conduct another full field layout inspection."

"Yes, sir," Lopez said with a half-grin.

Two days later, the barracks, with a new coat of paint inside top-to-bottom and scrubbed to a high luster, as were the troopers occupying it, passed Colonel Kingston's inspection with flying colors.

Colonel Kingston looked across the conference table at me and said, "Captain Bendell, you are in charge of the Group's classified documents and area studies?"

"Yes, sir," I replied.

"I want the area studies on every country in Africa totally updated," he said. "I'll want to start reading some in a few weeks."

"Yes, sir," I replied, thinking how badly I wanted to be back at Dak Pek.

As the S-3 started giving his report, I looked down at a bandage over a cut on my finger. I had been bow-hunting again and nicked my finger on one of the razor-sharp broadhead hunting arrows.

I thought back to my two bows at Dak Pek in 1968. I had my then-wife buy and mail me a Bear Kodiak Magnum bow and hunting arrows, but before they arrived, I bought the same thing on the black market in Kontum. I had two bows and two sets of arrows, along with bow quivers, shooting gloves, and wrist guards, there in Vietnam.

I screwed field tip points into the ends of the aluminum shafts and set targets up on the sandbags around ammo bunkers and practiced. One day, I stopped a couple of Montagnards who were hunting rats with their bamboo crossbows. I set up a Lucky Strike cigarette on a sandbag, and we stood off about thirty feet or so. I drew an arrow back and held at my anchor point on the edge of my jaw. I took a breath, let it out halfway, made sure my mouth was closed, and let the string slip off my first three fingers. *Twang, swoosh, thump.* The arrow vibrated out of the sandbag only two inches from the cigarette. I threw my shoulders back with pride and gave the two Jeh Montagnard hunters a cocky grin.

One said something to the other that I couldn't hear, and they both laughed heartily.

"My bang," I said impatiently, telling the first to shoot.

He loaded a bamboo bolt onto the tiny homemade crossbow. Both bows were already cocked. He took quick aim and fired, and the little cigarette split right in half. The second man fired and nicked the short end of the cigarette as it lay on the lip of one sandbag.

"Son of a bitch," I said, totally amazed.

The first warrior said, *"Trung-uy, my wa chiu ao, hutt nhia?"*

"Oh, luy liem jai," I replied enthusiastically.

This idiot had just invited an active alcoholic to go drink rice wine with them. I loved it. Three pee breaks later, I was feeling just fine, thank you very much, and we started talking about the tiger.

Dak Pek had been plagued in recent months by a man-eating tiger. Just a week before, it had grabbed a woman out harvesting mountain rice and dragged her into the jungle. She was from the village of Dak Peng Sial Peng Set, south of the camp proper. We had checked our back-trail on one of my operations and found tiger tracks where he had followed our patrol and finally gone off the side of the ridgeline. Judging from his saucer-size tracks, he was big.

Things had been slow for a few days, which was miraculous for Dak Pek, so I went to the A-team CO and asked to take a squad-size patrol out and patrol along the banks of the Dak Pek River. It was the smaller of the two main rivers in the valley, the main one being the Dak Poko. It was also where the tiger had been spotted most often.

My best friend was the camp's chief interpreter, named Nhual. Sometimes I called him Ba Nua, which means "Father of Nua," the name his closest friends also used for him.

Like most Montagnard men, Nhual was short, well muscled, and copper-skinned. He had black hair with a red streak from a childhood bout of malnutrition. He was extremely intelligent and was very intrigued by just about anything new. He had grown up speaking the Jeh language but had learned to speak English and Vietnamese fluently. This would not have been so amazing except for the fact that he had never been to school a day in his life. Like other Montagnards, Nhual had grown up eating bats, rats, and monkeys and wearing a loincloth, brass bracelets, and brass earrings. He carried a bamboo crossbow and lived in the jungle in Vietnam's mountainous Central Highlands region, north of the triborder area of Cambodia, Laos, and Vietnam. He even learned to play the guitar from one of the previous sergeants at Dak Pek.

Nhual assembled a squad-size patrol, not counting my bodyguards. During the summer of 1968, Y Bham Enuol issued orders that made me a brigadier general in the FULRO, in charge of the Jeh. After that occurred, six bodyguards, some of the toughest fighters in the valley, shadowed me. I hadn't asked for them; they were just assigned to me. The rule they followed was simple: If I got captured or killed, each of them would be put to death immediately. I don't know why, but for them being a bodyguard for me was an honor.

Things got quite hairy for those around me, and for me too at times. I had a beautiful Jeh woman I loved, who drank poisoned whiskey in my bunker one day and almost died. It had been meant for me. Fortunately, the medic and the doctors at the hospital saved her life. A little Montagnard girl named Plar, whose parents had been killed by the VC, wanted me to adopt her. I wanted to and had gotten the necessary paperwork, but the Vietnamese raped and murdered her and tossed her body into the barbed wire in our perimeter.

One night, our engineer/demo man, Larry Crotsley, and I were sitting on sandbags above my bunker talking. When I lit a cigarette, someone in my camp put six rounds from an M-16 on automatic over our heads, snatching the beret off of my head. One day, I unloaded a C7A Caribou on the camp runway, a grenade dropped into the gas tank of the jeep I was driving, a rubber band around the flipper. The grenade exploded at the end of the runway while I was driving and almost killed me.

One night when I was on radio watch in the team house, a cluster-bomb-unit booby trap with a tripwire was placed in front of the door. It almost got me when I walked out the door, but luckily I spotted the tripwire at the last millisecond. A Rade who was a trainer for the FULRO came to Dak Pek for a few weeks and was poisoned and killed by the Vietnamese.

Another friend from FULRO was beaten to death with clubs one night. We had been having a camp celebration, and I had been invited to drink that day at numerous Montagnards' bunkers. Nhual and my bodyguards stayed sober and kept their eyes on two Vietnamese hit men who had been hired to kill me and was following me all over the camp that day. That night, while I was drinking with the head of our all-Montagnard recon platoon, several members of the recon platoon grabbed the two Vietnamese, took them out in the jungle, and executed them both. I found out from the FULRO, who also kept Montagnard spies working in and near the Vietnamese, that the Vietnamese barber we had hired for the camp from Kontum was in fact a hit man, a known hit man, brought in by the Vietnamese to kill me. We were sure he was the one who had poisoned the whiskey in my bunker. I gave him an "earcut" with my large Montagnard knife, and as the late author Louis L'Amour used to say, "I then read to him from the book." He ran to our runway and hopped aboard a C7A Caribou that was being unloaded, grabbed a cable near the cockpit, and refused to let go or get off the aircraft. One of the guys on the team contacted me about it, and I told him to let him leave, without a pass, ID papers, or luggage. A FULRO messenger riding on the aircraft back to Kontum carried a message about the hit man to FULRO members in Kontum. He didn't kill any more people.

The men with my patrol were armed with a Browning automatic rifle, M-2 carbines, and M-79 grenade launchers; Nhual carried an M-16 rifle, and every man had hand grenades. I, the mighty hunter Bendell, was armed with only my Bear hunting bow and arrows. This was how we set off to bravely pursue the man-eating tiger. Hey, I might enjoy bow-hunting, but I'm not totally stupid. If I could have brought a tank along for extra backup, I would have.

Prior to leaving, I met with the CO and the team sergeant and worked out a small AO, or area of operations, to cover that bounded the Dak Pek to the southwest of the camp.

We left at daybreak. By ten in the morning, we had actually discovered some tracks of the tiger. The tracks only crossed the trail, though, and went down the side of the mountain through the thick jungle undergrowth.

It would have been totally impossible for even the most expert of trackers to follow tracks in that jungle. It is very hard for anybody who has not been there to actually understand the type of terrain we operated in all the time. Many of the mountains were so steep that to climb them we literally stepped on tiny tree trunks like ladder rungs. Most of the time, our point men had to chop and hack through very thick undergrowth with machetes to clear a path.

The triple canopy jungle was so thick, allowing so little daylight to penetrate, it was almost like night in many places. The layers of leaf and branch cover were so thick that regular artillery rounds would explode high up in the trees. Whenever I called in artillery, I asked for VT fuses. Variable timing fuses on artillery rounds caused them to explode a short time after the actual impact. Normally, this type of round was used to penetrate bunkers and other structures before exploding. When going through the thick tangle of leaves, vines, and branches, however, the round exploded above the ground with an airburst.

The undergrowth consisted of various grasses, plants, flowers, bushes, and branches; leaves such as elephant ears that were very large and thick; and vines. In many places it was so thick that firefights with the enemy were less than twenty or thirty feet apart. Quite often during a firefight you would see muzzle flashes from North Vietnamese guns just a few feet away, but you would never see the soldiers themselves.

Besides the steep mountains and ridges, thick tree cover, and dense undergrowth, the jungles around Dak Pek were filled with malaria-carrying anopheles mosquitoes; deadly snakes like cobras, banded kraits, bamboo vipers, and pythons; elephants; tigers; deadly bugs; booby traps; NVA; VC; numerous diseases; lots of rabid animals; unexpended ordnance; and maybe even things that go bump in the night. Other than that, it was absolutely beautiful, wonderful country.

The NVA and VC used some trails over and over again, but most of the time they tried to use different routes so they wouldn't establish a pattern. Sometimes they walked down the middle of streams after dark, trying to avoid ambushes by Americans. Most of the trails the Vietnamese used followed ridgelines and grew over quickly if they were not used on a daily basis.

On our second day, we were walking along one of these ridgelines when we were given the signal to stop, and I was summoned forward to our three-man point patrol.

When I returned to our men, I ordered them to turn and backtrail where we had already walked. The reason I had them do this was that the North Vietnamese and especially the local VC would sometimes follow our larger operations just to see what we were up to, or pick off any small patrols we left behind. I figured that the point had picked up sign of someone following us. I was almost right.

I could see out over the valley of the Dak Poko to the northeast. I was looking directly over the tops of tall trees growing on the mountainside below me. This particular ridgeline was pretty clear, and the trail had been heavily used by NVA coming in from Laos, which I could see a few miles off to the west. The camp of Dak Pek was clearly visible, and I wondered how many enemy soldiers had been down this trail and looked at the camp while I was there walking from the shower to my bunker, or drinking a can of beer outside the teamhouse door, or whatever.

I knew something was amiss as I approached the point. The youngest member of the three—a young man married for twelve years, now on his first operation— looked at me with eyes like saucers and his face a little lacking in color. Nhual and I knelt down with the leader of the point patrol, and my heart leaped as I saw the hard, black, wet mud of the mountaintop trail. The tiger's tracks were large—very large.

They were on top of the numerous footprints left by the men in my patrol, but what was more unnerving was the fact that we got up and followed the tracks back farther and discovered the tiger had been following us for more than a kilometer, or around six-tenths of a mile. We decided to return to where we found the tracks. We got to the spot where I first knelt down and saw that the tracks had gone off the trail and down the mountainside toward Dak Pek.

Nhual and I rejoined the rest of the patrol and had the point get with us and become the rear guard. I decided to cover the rest of the AO and set up a perimeter for the night. Tomorrow we would return to camp. I had to fill out my report for the MOPSUM, the monthly operational summary for the A-team.

The MOPSUM was simply another tool, in my opinion, for those of us at A-detachments. Each man on the team had a part of the report to fill out, so that the "Chairborne Rangers" in some air-conditioned office at higher headquarters could look it over and say important things like "Hey, Dak Pek still has fifty-two thirty-caliber machine guns," and "Dak Pek has seven fifty-caliber machine guns, and they are only authorized two. How come?" I always wondered who thought up the idea of these reports, as each one was just one more chance for a Viet Cong hooch-duster, laundress, cook, driver, interpreter, or mistress employed by Americans at headquarters to find out what we were doing and what our strengths and weaknesses were.

Being smart, most of us had learned to lie like a motherfucker when it came to listing our strengths and weaknesses. In fact, we did have fifty-two thirty-caliber machine guns at Dak Pek, but we only reported the fourteen we were authorized. We only reported the two authorized fifties, although we had seven.

When Joe Dietrich became A-team commander in the late summer of 1968, the B-team CO sent down a directive to make sure that fifty percent of our personnel on the A-team were always out on operations. On paper, that might look nice, but a Vietnam Operational Detachment-A was authorized only fourteen personnel. Each team was supposed to have two officers and ten enlisted men, just like a normal twelve-man team, but in Vietnam a civil affairs/psychological operations officer and an NCO were added. At home on the eleven o'clock news, they didn't show civil affairs efforts such as having churches send clothing for Montagnard children, giving medical aid to villagers, or building churches. At home on the news, they only liked to show us killing people or burning down villages, which were what the enemy used as military bases.

I wondered where the big cat was headed and thought about him scouting us after dark. It was so dark in the jungle at night, you couldn't possibly see a thing. He could smell us, but we were at a loss, or at least I was. The Montagnards couldn't smell the enemy, but they must have sensed them somehow because they always knew when they were near. I hoped they could do the same with a man-eating tiger. I felt very exposed when I slept in the jungle.

In Special Forces we traveled very light, and my routine for sleep on an operation was always the same. Before dark, I had all my men dig foxholes and get into them. That was for the benefit of any VC or NVA watching. After dark, they all moved and dug their real night positions. Somewhere near the center of our perimeter, I would find two small trees about eight feet apart. I carried a nylon hammock in my right hip pocket that had parachute suspension line attached to both ends. I tied off one end to one tree and then tugged and pulled on the other end, tying it to the other tree. Next, I pitched a roof over my tight little bed with an Army poncho, with suspension line attached to each corner and around the hood.

Following that, I would find a large forked stick and stick it into the ground next to the hammock. I would hang my BAR ammo belt and harness on that and my CAR-15 rifle, which is a sawed-off M-16 rifle with a telescoping stock. I carried the BAR harness and ammo pouches, as I could stick three M-16 magazines upside down and one crosswise on top of it in each of the pouches. I also kept a Kaybar knife taped upside down on the harness, as well as canteens, Army field dressing bandage, and some HE and smoke grenades. In this case, however, I didn't have the harness—just a big two-quart bladder canteen; a belt and quick-draw holster; a Smith & Wesson .357 Magnum; and my Bear Kodiak Magnum hunting bow with a rubber Quickee Kwiver bow quiver mounted on it, filled with thirty-one-inch Easton aluminum arrows, and topped with Satellite four-blade broadhead hunting arrows. I also hung the little CIDG rucksack I carried, which contained one extra pair of socks, LRRP-ration dehydrated meals, salt pills, medical supplies, extra canteens, and extra ammunition.

Next to the forked stick I would insert two shorter sticks into the ground and hang my jungle boots upside down on them. This was simply to let them air and dry out during the night and prevent creepy crawlers from climbing into their warm and smelly recesses.

When I was ready for bed, I would spread the tight little hammock sides apart and lie down, putting on a little pair of mosquito-net mittens and head net, which I had purchased at a sporting goods store in Fayetteville, North Carolina, before going to "the big rifle range across the pond." I carried these folded up in my left hip pocket. I wrapped up in my Army poncho liner.

In SF you always travel light, so we wore the same uniform day in and day out on operations, changing only our socks occasionally. The uniform was a camo tiger suit and jungle boots, and I wore a camo cowboy hat and black cowboy scarf, which could be used as a triangular bandage or as an expedient gag or handcuffs for a prisoner. The heat and humidity were so bad, nobody wore underwear in

'Nam. I carried my toothbrush in my right trouser-leg cargo pocket and brushed while crossing streams. We didn't shave or bathe on operations.

If the tiger wanted to stalk us that evening and was to consider taking a bite out of me while I lay helpless at tiger's-mouth height, maybe, just maybe, my rank odor would drive him away. In fact, getting a good whiff of myself right then, I decided any sensible tiger would run all the way to Laos to get away from my body odor. I did wonder what would be on his mind that evening.

A strange sound was coming from the mouths of the two-legged creatures that were such easy prey. The sound was the Jeh word for tiger, *bumom,* and this large creature had heard that sound many times. The creatures roared with that sound in high screams whenever the *bumom* took a prey from a mountain ricefield, or along a bank of the big fast-moving water. He preferred taking them at the jungle's edge near the ricefields because he hated the water, but he took them when and where he could.

This night, as I later envisioned it, the big cat raised his orange and black head, testing the air. His mind catalogued the various scents coming on the nighttime breeze. There were the smells of cook fires, rice, flowers, bamboo and trees, water, human perspiration, feces, urine, menses, and semen, cooking rat and monkey, dead dog, steel, gunpowder, water buffalo, and the decaying corpse of a dead NVA soldier in the jungle across the valley, two miles distant.

The big tiger looked at the side-by-side villages of Dak Jel Kong and Dak Jel Luk and chose the former. It was farther away from the nearby Special Forces camp of Dak Pek with its many smells of gunpowder and steel—real danger instincts to the big cat.

He crouched low as he left the relative safety of the

jungle's cover and moved through the moonlight toward the Montagnard village. It would soon be dawn, and he instinctively knew that some of the two-legged creatures would come out into the mountain ricefields at the jungle's edge. He would stretch out near the field and wait. If the wind shifted, the big cat would keep getting up and moving, so the wind always came from the village and the ricefields to his nostrils. He didn't reason any of this out or catalog the smells by reasoning. Instead, it all came to him instinctively.

It was close to dawn, and my eyes popped open. As always, I lay still at first and just listened in the darkness. My ears strained to hear beyond the constant buzzing of the mosquitoes flying all around my head net. I scratched my right cheek, where the head net had fallen against my skin and many of the little pests had sucked my blood. I stretched my arms out and yawned, as false dawn turned the sky to gray.

The tiger lay among some tall green shafts of bamboo, and his eyes popped open. As always, he listened without moving, and his always-powerful nostrils tested the wind again, checking to see if any prey or enemy were near. He licked a bamboo nick on his left volleyball-size paw and stretched his mighty legs out, yawning. Then the big cat got up and walked slowly through the grasses looking for a spot to urinate and make a scratch.

As the sky lightened, I climbed out of the jungle hammock and removed my mittens and head mask. I lit a Lucky Strike and walked about five feet away from my hammock and relieved my bladder. One of my bodyguards knelt by my ammo harness and rucksack and grinned up at me from the small smokeless fire he had going in a foot-deep hole. My canteen cup had been soaped on the outside to keep it from being permanently blackened, and he now had the cup full of boiling water so I could start the morning out with hot tea, coffee, or cocoa.

A second canteen cup would be boiled so I could pour it into a plastic bag of dehydrated chili con carne—my favorite—spaghetti, chicken stew, or whatever. I sipped a cup of steaming-hot tea and lit up another cigarette. A hacking cough bringing phlegm up out of my twenty-two-year-old lungs. I wanted a drink badly.

The tiger trotted through two miles of thick, unforgiving jungle to get a drink of water from a stream. After drinking, he climbed a tall, steep ridge and crossed over it because the wind had shifted. His muscles rippled with each powerful step.

Twenty miles away, a female tiger was coming into estrus, and it wouldn't be long before the big male's wanderings brought him to the smell of her almost on the run.

I looked out over the treetops below my eye level and at the distant camp and surrounding villages. I thought of my beautiful Montagnard lover. She would be lying nude on my bed in my bunker, drinking a cup of hot coffee with tons of sugar and cream in it.

On his way back to the ricefield, the big cat came across the trail of a herd of wild pigs heading north through the jungle. He began trailing them, forgetting about the two-legged creatures. Instinct would later bring him back to Dak Pek again and again.

The sound of one of my listening posts firing brought all of us into our gear with weapons locked, loaded, and ready to fight. A VC unit was hitting a Yard striker who was stuck out there alone, sixty meters out to the south of us along the trail.

I crawled toward the noise with Nhual at my side. "We gotta save his ass, Ba Nua," I said. "Tell the men to get up here next to us."

Nhual relayed my instructions in Jeh. My six body-guards had been all around me the whole time, and the rest of the patrol now assembled around me. I instructed one, a fire team–size element, to sweep along the side of the ridge toward the west, while the rest swept across the top of the ridgeline and moved rapidly toward the man stuck on the trail.

I tried to figure out how big the VC unit was. The firing was sporadic now, and I could hear no automatic weapons. Small-arms battles always sound much larger than they really are, so I had to try to slow my metabolism so I could think clearly. Time to get scared later. I figured that the man had ambushed maybe a squad-size unit and it sounded like the two enemy groups were potshotting toward each other with searching fire. Because there were no sounds of automatic-weapons fire except his M-2 carbine, I hoped it was just a small number of local VC.

Around Dak Pek, a permanent group of about two companies-minus of local VC had been forcefully recruited from the local villages by their North Vietnamese cadre, who threatened to rape and kill the women and children of each participating village if the men didn't fight for them. Therefore the local VC were somewhat of a joke, as their hearts were not into fighting us. I knew who most of these VC were and often ate and got drunk with them in their villages. It wasn't spoken aloud that I knew they were VC or that they knew I knew, but it was kind of a mutual understanding.

Oddly, I never felt fear in the villages because of my standing with the FULRO. Any Jeh who killed me would have the other Jeh to fear—not the VC, NVA, South Vietnamese, or American—and none of the local ragtags wanted that. I didn't feel sorry for these starving wounded men, either, because some of the villages stood up to the

North Vietnamese threats of recrimination, but these villages didn't and the men had all lost their pride, which was about all the Vietnamese had not taken away from the Montagnards. We went out of our way to protect the villages and villagers who stood up to the enemy, and the men in those villages were awesome fighters filled with warrior spirit and self-esteem. Afraid to attack them too often, the local VC and NVA went to the sympathizing villages more often and simply drained them dry of everything. It was much easier.

My immediate reaction, tactically, was that the VC would go off the west side of the ridge, away from Dak Pek, where the indirect-fire weapons from the camp would have less of a chance to find them out while they retreated. One fire team swept the top of the mountain, while the other went forward on an angle, hoping to catch the enemy unit in almost a crossfire.

We reached the lone Yard striker within minutes. He was hiding behind a large tree next to the trail with a large pile of expended thirty-caliber shells lying all around him. He had had a busy morning thus far and probably hadn't had a chance yet to take a crap while perusing *The Wall Street Journal.*

I saw a blink of light far down the trail and fired a broadhead arrow at it, not knowing if it would find a target or not. Off to my right, some Yards opened up with carbines and the BAR, but within a minute the jungle was completely still.

Besides Luckies, I smoked Swisher Sweet cigarillos in those days, always trying to live up to the silly nickname, Clint Eastwood, that our first senior radio operator had comically given to me—a wonderful guy who was killed right before going on R and R. I pulled one of my little cigars out and stuck it into the smiling mouth of the Yard defender and lit it for him. That was all he needed in the way of appreciation. You could see it in his beaming eyes.

He joined Nhual and me as we went forward. I saw a black-pajamaed figure lying on the ground writhing in pain and thought how great it would be to have a prisoner and get some current intelligence. My enthusiasm was short-lived, however, as my largest bodyguard bent over the enemy soldier and, before I could yell, slit his throat. His body twitched.

In those days I always covered up and buried all stress, duress, fear, rage, and sensitivity I felt beneath a macho facade of bravado and humor. Anything else would have shown vulnerability, in my mind.

I lit my own cigar and grinned at Nhual, clenching it between my teeth. "Hey," I said, "somebody should have told him he shouldn't be a Communist if he can't take a fucking joke."

Nhual said, "You are very pissed, huh? You wanted a live prisoner."

I laughed, then got serious and stared out over the valley. "Yeah, but what else is new? There's no such thing as having NVA or VC prisoners when you have Jeh strikers at the same time. Tell this man he is very brave and that I am honored to fight at his side."

Nhual relayed the words while we walked up to the dead body wearing tattered black pajamas. It was an NVA, and his cohorts had carried off the AK-47 that he never got a chance to fire. His little pack was still on his back, though, so we checked it out. Inside was mildewed rice, an American CBU, or cluster bomb unit, that he apparently was going to use to make a booby trap, an old picture of a very ugly Vietnamese woman, and some loose 7.62-millimeter rounds.

This told us a lot. The Yard defender told Nhual that

the others in the squad were local Yards, most from Dak Long Nhang, the southeasternmost village in the valley. The dead man had been a North Vietnamese adviser to the local yokels, and he looked gaunt and undernourished. Well, right then he looked quite dead and bloody, too, but his predeath condition seemed to be very poor. His clothing and supplies indicated that the local VC had had their shit flapping in the breeze.

I looked at the tattered picture of the man's wife, mother, or whatever and commented to Nhual, "No wonder this poor fucker was down here living with our local VC. If I had an old lady this ugly, I would find the worst jungle in the world to hide in, too. She looks like she tests out the sharpness of punji stakes with her face."

The latter comment had to be explained more clearly to Nhual, but he translated and all the strikers shared a big laugh. One of the Yards cut the dead soldier's left ear off and stuck it into his pocket as we saddled up and prepared to head back to camp. My men were pumped, and I only wished that I was a coach and they were going to play for me in the Super Bowl.

Nhual decided to make his own joke and pointed at the man who had collected the dead man's ear. "He makes potato chips," he said.

It was my turn to laugh. "Let's go home," I said.

Being a civil affairs/psychological operations officer, I felt I had to do my duty. I pulled a *chieu hoi* pass out of my pack.

Chieu hoi passes are small leaflets that were most often dropped from aircraft over trails, especially the Ho Chi Minh Trail. They instructed the NVA or VC that they could surrender, without recrimination or fear, by simply raising their hands and yelling, *"Chieu hoi! Chieu hoi!"*

In that case, they would not be treated as prisoners of

war but would be taken to a Chieu Hoi Center, where they would be reeducated on how wonderful the Saigon government was. It was an excellent way for NVA or VC to take a two- or three-week vacation, get well fed and clothed, and fill up on new intelligence about the enemy—us. They would then take off from the Chieu Hoi Center and rejoin their unit.

I had found a better use for the Chieu Hoi leaflets. I pulled my grease pencil out of my left trouser cargo pocket and wrote: *"Ho Chi Minh is an ugly, bearded fucking pussy. Yours very truly, Lieutenant Bendell (Clint Eastwood), Dak Pek."*

I stuck the leaflet into the dead NVA soldier's open mouth and, chuckling, pulled out a Swisher Sweet, sticking it unlit in my parched mouth. Nhual told the patrol what I was doing, and they all laughed. None of them saw me, however, slip the old photograph of the ugly woman under the corpse's black PJs. I placed it on his frail lifeless chest, just above his heart.

Later that night, I sat at the felt-topped poker table in our new team house. We had made the table out of rocks from the Dak Poko River, concreted in and covered with a felt-covered plywood octagonal table top. I played poker with several guys on the team while slurping a glass of whiskey and drinking a Budweiser beer.

"That woman was so ugly, Commo Willy," I commented, "I wouldn't fuck her with your dick."

Everyone laughed.

The assistant medic asked, "Where is the picture, Lieutenant?"

"I must have dropped it in the jungle," I said, and my face took on a strange sober cast.

One of the sergeants said, "Well, it might keep the

NVA for a while if you dropped it on a trail where they can see it."

Everyone laughed, and I thought about how beautiful she must have looked to that dead Communist soldier. I suddenly noticed that I had been laughing hard, too. I folded my cards and retreated to my bunker and into the arms of my lover.

Two days later, I was sent to Dak To to try to recruit more Montagnards for our force of strikers. The XO of our sister camp, Dak Seang, would meet me there the following day. An order had come down from higher headquarters to recruit more Montagnards for our camp forces in all the A-camps.

The first night, as usual, I got quite drunk. I had been a teenage alcoholic, starting at the age of fifteen with binge drinking, and by this time I was a daily drunk with a tremendous capacity for booze on my skinny little frame. I had made friends with a captain from Dak To, and he introduced me to an MP captain whom I also befriended. We went out to a Vietnamese whorehouse and busted the young Americans there but shared a few drinks afterward with the Vietnamese hookers.

After that, we went to a large semisandbagged Quonset hut that apparently served as the officers' club for the First Brigade of the Fourth Infantry Division at Dak To. I was well into my cups when my friends took me in there to watch the night's feature film, *The Green Berets*, starring John Wayne.

I enjoyed the film and naturally got quite emotional. Up until then that evening, I had been funny, cheerful, and silly. Up until then, however, I had not heard any leg majors from any nonairborne units putting down Special Forces.

In the Army you do not wear "cover"—a hat—indoors, so when I had entered the makeshift O-club, I had removed my beret and tucked it into the cargo trouser pocket on my leg. We sat in the front row. As soon as the show ended, a Fourth Division major made some smart-aleck comments about Special Forces.

I jumped up as if I had been fired straight up out of a 155 Howitzer. I slammed my beret on my head, making sure the Fifth Group flash was over my left eye, two fingers' width above the eyebrow. It wasn't just another hat to me.

Drunkenly, I screamed, "You motherfucking leg, how dare you say shit about SF! You couldn't make a come drop on our leg, you chickenshit, steel-potted, pot-bellied, overloaded ground-humping pussy! You're all a bunch a chickenshit pussy legs! I'll fight you all, you pussies! Come on!"

Between their uproarious laughs, my two friends grabbed me by both arms and quickly pulled me backward out the door. They got me out in the cool of the night and started talking sense to me while moving me quickly away from there.

"Son of a bitch, Bendell," the MP captain said. "Besides that guy being a major, there was another major and a lieutenant colonel or two in there, along with a basic load of captains, lieutenants, and warrants."

"Fuck 'em!" I said. "They shouldn't fuck with SF. I'll kick all their fucking leg asses."

I awakened in the back of a three-quarter-ton truck, lying atop a pile of cloth bags. My mouth felt as if it had been used to lick the felt off an dirty old pool table. My head felt like the inside of a four-deuce mortar tube during a full-scale offensive. I started to get up, and my body felt as if I had just made a thousand-foot rappel with a hundred-foot rope.

I found a jeep nearby, so I hopped in and drove it over to the runway. Checking my Seiko from Kontum, I saw it was about time for the Dak Seang lieutenant to arrive. A Huey showed up less than five minutes later with him on it, wearing a rice wine hangover to match my own. Like me, he wore about ten brass Montagnard bracelets on each wrist. We sounded like a pair of wind chimes when we walked.

I mentioned to him about my "borrowed" vehicle, so he suggested we find him one, too. He handed me a big bottle from his overnight pack, and we drank rice wine driving around the First Brigade, Fourth Division headquarters area. Spotting another unattended jeep, I stopped, and he hopped out and "borrowed" it. After the previous night's drinking, it took only that shared bottle of rice wine to get us both plastered again. We drag-raced along the tarmac at Dak To runway and stopped at the end.

He pulled out a map, where we saw the Jeh villages marked north of the Fourth Division HQ. We took off with the jeeps and drag-raced each other along the dirt road. A pair of MPs stopped us at a checkpoint and told us the Yard villages were off-limits, as they were in enemy-controlled area.

"Sergeant," I said, "don't worry. We are on a top secret mission and I cannot discuss it, but we are cleared to go there."

"Sir," the MP said carefully, "I'm sorry, but that's not good enough to let you go."

"Sergeant," I whispered back, "can you keep your fucking mouth shut?"

"Yes, sir," he replied emphatically.

I said, "I'm only going to say two words, and I don't want you to say another word: Phoenix Program."

He got a startled look on his face, gave the other MP a nod, and let us pass.

As I took off by him, he said seriously, "Good luck, sir."

The other lieutenant and I were involved somewhat with the Phoenix Program in our respective areas, but right now we were just going out to recruit some Yards for our camps. As soon as we were out of sight of the MPs, we pulled over and agreed to split whoever we recruited.

A short time later, we found ourselves sitting around a large crock of rice wine with the chiefs of several villages. They had gotten together for a neighborly drinking bash and were already as potted as we were.

Drinking Montagnard rice wine is an art form, in a sense. They ferment rice in a large earthenware crock. When it's time for serious drinking, a bamboo stick is laid across the top of the pot. In the middle of that stick, another bamboo stick goes straight down several inches into the crock. A small hollow bamboo tube sticks down the middle of the crock, and a rubber siphon tube is attached to the top of that. The drinkers are seated in a circle around the giant crock.

When a drinker is ready, a woman comes up and fills the pot with water to the brim. The drinker then has to siphon wine out without removing the tube from his lips. If he removes the tube, more water is poured in and he must start over. He also has to drink until the wine level drops below the downward pointing stick. If he doesn't, the giant jug is filled to the top again, and he starts over. If you drink quickly, you get drunk quickly, but if you drink slowly, the rice swells and the fluid level keeps rising and you end up drinking more booze. Some rice wine tasted like dirty water. Some had rat tails and other niceties stirred in for good measure. Some tasted real smooth—in fact, most rice wine tasted real smooth, but it all knocked you flat on your ass.

The Yards are quite competitive, so before long the other louey and I challenged all the village chiefs to a drinking contest. If we won, they would move every man, woman, and child in their villages to our two camps, where the men would join our strike forces. To win, we would have to drink until we passed out or they did. If we lost, we would give them our jeeps.

Before long, there were two village chiefs passed out, but the rest of us were going strong. The host chief's ugly old wife came up and siphoned rice wine out into chugging bowls. She filled each bowl halfway, then she poured bottles of Bier LaRue into each bowl and mixed it with the wine. We drank bowl after bowl.

It got to the point where I was so drunk that I would stand up, turn around, and relieve my bladder in place, while the Montagnard women would point at my short-comings and giggle.

The one thing the old chiefs overlooked was the fact that although the other lieutenant and I were thin, we both stood about six foot two. Most of them were under five foot four, so we had a whole lot more places in our bodies to absorb the liquor. It took the whole morning and after-noon, but finally they all passed out drunk.

I can remember the whole drinking contest and visit to the village, which is odd because I used to have horrible alcoholic blackouts and have no memory of days at a time. He and I got up and waved to the women, who were still laughing and giggling, and we drove away, with a promise to return the next morning for all the villagers. I remember leaving the village by drag racing back toward Dak To, but

I cannot remember where we slept or what happened from that time on. I do not know if we made it back to Dak To or slept in the jeeps or what. I just know that we returned the next day and several hundred Montagnard men, women, and children were walking along the dirt road toward Dak To. Most Yard tribes had no word in their language for *lying*, so these proud men wouldn't think of welching on their deal. We told them we would meet them at the runway, then turned around and headed back to do some scrounging.

Whenever any member of our team or any other A-team left site, we were to scrounge food and other goodies for the camp. The lieutenant and I raced around Dak To in our stolen jeeps lining up ice cream and other foodstuffs and whatever else we could find for our camps. We drove these to the runway, where we had a pair of giant Chinook helicopters lined up to take us to our camps. I do not know when or how we lined up the Chinooks, but apparently we did. We took several jeeploads of scrounged supplies to the choppers, then started picking up Yards and ferrying them to the big birds. When we finally assembled the Yard villagers, we first asked who wanted to go to Dak Seang and who wanted to go to Dak Pek. That didn't work because almost everyone wanted to go to Dak Pek since it was much bigger and more secure. Dak Pek was situated on a series of hills, officially about seven but unofficially about eleven. Anyway, the A-camp had barbed wire, tank traps, punji stakes, buried drums of fugas, and other goodies in perimeters around each hill, with a giant tank trap around the whole thing. On top of that, each hill was mutually supported by direct fire from at least two other hills.

Dak Seang was more like the stereotypical A-camp shown in *The Green Berets*. We divided the people up, keeping them in their family units, and Dak Seang ended up getting maybe three more people than Dak Pek. The villages had simply been deserted and left to the VC or whatever.

The giant rotors cranked up on the big twin CH-47 Chinook helicopters, and we waited until the birds had time to warm up and go through their checklist. The remaining Yards loaded up, and we lifted off, heading north toward our tentative homes. The jeeps were left on the runway to hopefully be recovered by the units who had involuntarily lent them to us.

I had been hearing about an old-time SF sergeant major back at Fort Bragg on Smoke Bomb Hill. Very few people know how much power a sergeant major who has been around a bit has. The story was going around among SFers that this sergeant major was definitely SF, very professional, and had been a snake-eater for years.

A smartass E-4 was constantly going AWOL from this sergeant major's company. Before the last time, the old NCO had told him he better not do it again and fuck up his morning report again.

Supposedly the E-4 went AWOL again, got caught, and was brought back to meet with the company commander.

When he came before the sergeant major, he bragged, "Top, as soon as I get a chance, I'm going AWOL again."

The sergeant major grinned and said, "The fuck you are, young man. Not in my company."

With that, the old SF noncom pulled an Army Colt .45 automatic out of his drawer, aimed at the E-4's head, and fired. The sergeant major took great pride in the spit-polished floors of his company headquarters, so he shoved the man's head into a trash can to keep it from bleeding all over the shining tile. As the story goes, the whole incident was totally hushed up, except all kinds of SF people talked about it behind closed doors.

I pictured that major from Dak To who had put down Special Forces so bad after the movie, and I wondered if I could get him to visit the sergeant major with a note saying that he was going to go AWOL all the time. I watched the jungle and the winding Dak Poko River passing below us and couldn't wait to get home to Dak Pek. A week later, my friend at Dak To told me that that major had taken a direct hit, right on top of his helmet, by a sixty- or eighty-two-millimeter mortar round. They had to pour him into a body bag.

When I was told, I laughed. "Shouldn't fuck with SF if you can't take a fucking joke," I said.

We had a camp celebration to which I invited my two friends from the Fourth Division, the MP captain and an S-3 captain. It was a gala event for the Yards, and they were very excited about the preparations.

Four large bamboo poles had been carefully prepped and were buried, like giant fenceposts, in our camp parade ground in front of the LLVC team house. The outside of each pole was stripped down close to the ground with sharp knives. Each strip stayed connected to the pole and was then colored with various bright colors. It looked like fifteen-foot-high poles decorated with colored ribbons.

Next to the decorated poles, about a hundred folding chairs were set up in neat rows. Four giant crocks of *hutt nhiah,* rice wine, were set up on the chair side of the four poles. Four sacrificial cows were tied to the poles, and they stood baking alive in the unforgiving sun. The only relief they got was the wind coming off the wings of the tiny mosquitoes and flies buzzing around their reddish-brown hides.

After breakfast and the arrival of the visitors from Dak To, the Vietnamese Special Forces team, the LLDB—Luc Luong Dac Biet—and the U.S. Special Forces team were seated in the front row of chairs. Next came interpreters, the Americans from Dak To, families of LLDB, and then cadre members of the camp strike force and some of the local village chiefs.

Montagnard men assigned to various jobs stood by both ends of the rows of chairs, waiting anxiously to run out to carry on their duties. The camp strike force crowded around the whole scene, except for a skeleton force providing security around the perimeter.

The gongs started, as did the drums. A group of four Jeh men, wielding seven-foot-long spears and adorned with numerous brass bracelets, necklaces, ankle bracelets, and earrings, danced out onto the parade ground from behind the LLDB team house. Numerous Montagnards cheered and oohed and aahed as the Jeh danced out, raising spears and stabbing at imaginary enemies and quarry. Other dancers, mainly in the rear of the single-file line, were banging large brass gongs, and still others beat bamboo drums. The line marched closer and closer to the four cows, and four strikers, looking odd dressed in their normal uniforms, ran out and stood beside the cows, each holding an Army canteen cup in his hand.

Soon the four men carrying the long spears made their way to a spot to the right side of each cow. They danced around in place and made more stabbing gestures. Then, as if obeying some kind of silent signal, each man simultaneously jabbed his spear through the side of his cow. The long points of the bamboo spears penetrated all the way through the bodies of the full-grown cows and came out the other side. The men with the canteen cups then ran up and captured spurting blood from each cow's wound. They would fill a cup quickly and then run, blood overflowing all over their hands and sleeves, and pour the blood onto the crocks filled with rice wine. They would then run back to the dying animals and catch another cupful of blood and repeat the procedure.

After a few minutes and more stab wounds, the cows went to their knees and eventually their death.

We were brought forward to the crocks of rice wine, while the cows were quickly butchered and divided up between the families of the camp strike force. In less than five minutes the cows were totally gone and only small puddles of blood remained to seep into the camp parade ground. The Yards ate everything, including the hooves and genitalia, and I even saw one man carrying the hide to his bunker.

We crowded around the crocks of rice wine and drank sticks. Most of the guys on the team just drank a little and politely excused themselves to attend to their work, but I had to be sociable on this day. It was my job. I had received numerous invitations to go to different bunkers on this camp celebration day and share food and rice wine. The Montagnards were so poor and so many were so undernourished, it was indeed an honor to be asked to people's bunkers to share food and drink.

What was going to make the day harder—or easier, depending on how you looked at it—was the fact that I was already well on my way to being totally blitzed before I got up from the first crock of rice wine. I drank from all four crocks.

Nhual accompanied me, and I was also shadowed by my six ever-present bodyguards, who just stayed off a little bit. We first went to the bunker of my lover's aunt and uncle. Her parents had both been killed by the Viet Cong. The uncle had tried to rape her a number of times while she was growing up, but I visited out of politeness and respect for family—very important with the Yards. I drank one stick of rice wine, ate something gross, and bade them adieu.

Next we went to the bunker of a platoon leader in Charlie Company. The man was an outstanding fighter and had to wear a steel loincloth just to contain his brass balls. His wife was very pretty and had a set of breasts that Hugh Hefner would have paid a million dollars to showcase. The couple, in their early twenties, had had six children, but only one still lived. One had died from the bite of a banded krait, and the rest from various Third World–type diseases. We drank rice wine from a crock covered with elephant ear leaves in the corner of his bunker. It was obvious it had been saved for a special occasion.

I drank several sticks and went to his boss's bunker next. Mister Lon was fairly tall—in fact, not far from my six foot two. He was neither Montagnard nor Vietnamese. He was FULRO but was from one of the other three branches, the FLKN, the Front de Libération de Kambuja Nord or Liberation Front of Northern Cambodia. In other words, he was Khmer Krom, a Cambodian resistance fighter. Mister Lon had come to Dak Pek to escape from some people in Cambodia who hadn't taken kindly to his killing some of their leaders, and he wanted to get training and experience fighting along with American Special Forces.

On one of my first days of my first operation at Dak Pek, Mister Lon had been ballsy enough to play a trick on me, and I respected and liked the man. He had been eating some red and green hot peppers that were sitting in line on a log. We were on top of a mountain due west of Dak Pek, on a fire support base built earlier by the 101st Airborne.

At the time, we were providing flank security for elements of the First Brigade, Fourth Infantry Division.

To get water, we would have had to send patrols down the steep sides of the tall mountain we were on, so our water was hauled to us by chopper in the metal canisters that artillery rounds came in.

Lon was eating his peppers as if they were candy while talking to several strikers. I walked up with Suet, one of the camp interpreters, and asked Lon how hot the peppers were. He told me they weren't hot at all and were very mild. To prove his point, he popped several in his mouth and smiled broadly and continued talking while eating them.

He handed me one, which I tossed between my lips. I might as well have popped a hot coal in my mouth. I was on fire. It felt as if I had tried to swallow a cupful of molten lava, fresh from a volcanic eruption. I looked around, eyes watering, steam pouring out my ears. I spotted our water canisters, ran over to them, and unscrewed the top off one. I raised it up and literally drenched myself while swallowing as much water as I could. The assembled Yards laughed and laughed, along with Mister Lon.

Afterward, he came over and clasped my hand in genuine friendship while slapping a hand on my back. Other LLDB might have done the same thing to make me "lose face"—a big thing with them—but I could tell Lon was just having fun.

We went into his bunker, and I said hello to his wife. Lon didn't have rice wine. He had a bottle of moonshine whiskey and poured me an eight-ounce glass, handing me a can of Budweiser as a chaser. His wife brought us each a bowl of tiny chunks of cow's lungs, boiled in water.

When I started on my second glass of whiskey, I asked where he had gotten the booze from. Lon took me out into the now-blinding sunlight and to another bunker. Inside were several cheerful Yards happily making moonshine. The still had been made from the radiator of an Army deuce-and-a-half.

While Nhual and I were walking across the top of Lon's company hill, Nhual pointed out two Vietnamese men who had been following me all day. He informed me that they were professional killers, hit men hired by the LLDB to do me in because of the FULRO.

We left Lon's bunker and went to Bayh's bunker. Bayh was the head of the recon platoon and another major leader for the Jeh tribe. I stayed in Bayh's bunker, drinking, telling stories, eating dinner, and making plans until well after dark. In the meantime, Bayh called in two recon platoon strikers, who went outside, got a couple of my bodyguards, and made the two Vietnamese hitmen disappear permanently.

When I wanted to return to my bunker, Nhual assigned five Montagnards to literally carry me there, I was so drunk. I was placed in my bed sometime that night and awakened sometime the next day, week, or month—I think.

Joe Howard, a really good E-6 and our team intelligence sergeant, shared my bunker part of the time. My bunker was directly underneath our western sandbagged fifty-caliber-machine-gun bunker. When it was built, a hole had been dug about ten feet long by fifteen feet wide. Four steps were cut down off the wall of the four-deuce mortar pit, and the walls of the pit were cemented. Two firing ports were built into the side of the hole, from which Joe and I could fire our weapons if the camp were attacked. The roof was made of PSP—perforated steel plating—covered with plywood, then concrete, and the stand for the fifty was cemented in.

The bunker had a little plywood door, an overhead light bulb, and a plywood divider running the length of the underground room to separate Joe's side from mine.

After I returned from my first operation, the team sergeant, Master Sergeant Pickles, had been bitten on the foot by a large rat. Our medic had plenty of rabies medicine, and he had had to give Top the series of excruciating painful shots in his abdomen: one each day in a counter-clockwise direction for better than a week.

Several days later, Joe Howard, sleeping in our bunker, was bitten by another large rat. The next day, I had to help hold him down with another team member while he received his first abdominal shot from Bac-si. *Bac-si* is the Vietnamese word for doctor and the nickname given every SF medic.

A couple days after the camp celebration, I went into my bunker, shortly after Joe. I turned out the light, got into bed, and thought about the events of the day.

Quite often in those days, Special Forces men tried to outdrink and gross out other people. Those of us who were younger seemed to buy into a lot more than the older men, who simply had a great deal of pride in knowing that we were the best fighting force the world had ever seen, copied quite often but never duplicated.

Earlier in the day, we had been in the team house eating lunch, when the medic and assistant medic had come in the door, laughing uproariously.

These two men, like all A-team medics, were busier every day of the week than any two doctors in any emergency room anywhere in the world. They also treated very much the same injuries and diseases as any fully qualified doctor anywhere. The work they did was never-ending, dif-

ficult, and thankless. The only difference between these SF
medics and many ER doctors was that the SF medics got
shot at quite often, and they didn't get the salary or recog-
nition of a civilian doctor.

Like other SFers, medics worked hard and played
hard. The two medical men at Dak Pek were no different.

They were looking at a Polaroid photograph that one
medic was holding, and their laughter didn't subside—in
fact, the hilarity increased. Naturally, the outburst aroused
the curiosity of every man on the team, so we all crowded
around to look at the snapshot.

First the assistant medic explained: "This Montagnard
woman came into the dispensary this morning, and she had
a dead baby in her. She had started labor and the baby's
arm was hanging outside of her vagina, so Bac-si had me
take this picture."

We all looked at the photograph. It showed a close-up
of the woman's legs spread apart and the fetus's right arm
sticking out. Wearing his beret and flashing a big smile at
the camera, Bac-si was shaking hands with the dead baby.

We all laughed hilariously because that was what you
did in those days, at that place.

I think a little tiny voice was hidden somewhere inside
each of us that probably tried to cry out each day, many
times, over some new atrocity. The little voice could never
be heard, though, as it was hidden under layer after layer
of protective macho veneer. It probably is good that it
wasn't ever heard. I think that macho armor probably kept
us safe from our enemies and even our allies, the Vietnamese. I think they all thought we were a little off-balance,
and maybe that was a good frame of mind to keep them in.

I remember a dark night about two in the morning
when the medic at Dak Pek saved my life. He wasn't alone,
though. A dust-off helicopter had flown to my camp

through the highest mountains in Vietnam, and every A-camp between Kontum and Dak Pek had shot artillery flares up to form an alley of light for the chopper to follow in and out of our remote valley. I remember that night, but that's a different story altogether. There are plenty of Vietnam stories about the courage of dust-off helicopters and their crews.

"Captain Bendell, what's the story on the insurgency that started there?"

The words startled me and brought me out of my daydream. I stared into the steely-cold eyes of Colonel Kingston, the Third Herd CO, and looked for a hole to crawl into.

"Pardon me, sir," I heard myself finally say.

"I was asking you a fucking question, Captain, which to me was very important," the hard-core colonel said firmly. "Weren't you listening to me?"

"No, sir," I said flatly.

"Why not?"

"I fucked up, sir. I was daydreaming," I replied.

The straightforwardness and honesty shocked the old man for a second, but that was what was expected and respected in Special Forces. Fortunately, I had learned that early.

"What could you be daydreaming about that's more important than matters at hand, Captain?" he snapped.

I said, "Vietnam. The Montagnards. Dust-offs, sir."

A faint hint of a grin spread across the colonel's mouth.

8

Airborne Ambulance

I T WAS JULY 25, 1968, and I was busy fighting elements of the Twenty-fourth Regiment of the Second NVA Division on an operation due west of Dak Pek. Hundreds of miles to the south, Al Nichols, now a captain, was flying area coverage near Can Tho in the Mekong Delta.

Al's unit, out of Soc Trang, had six dust-offs, and three of them were in service all the time. One flew support for the Ninth Infantry Division. The second flew support for regional forces, and the third flew area coverage, responsible for medevac service anywhere in the IV Corps area.

On that particular day, Al had set his medevac down in a staging area not far from Sa Dec, where the Song Cua Tieu, Song Ham Luong, and Song Co Chein rivers all fork from the Song Tieng Giang. Along with the Song Hau Giang and minor tributaries, these three rivers form the mighty Mekong River, the aorta of South Vietnam.

Ever since the Tet Offensive earlier that year, the VC had been on a constant high and kept looking for new fixes of victory. They were also better supplied and much tougher.

On that fateful July day, Al got a call to fly out and rescue a wounded American RTO, or radio carrier, along with an FO, a MAC-V artillery forward observer attached to an ARVN battalion that was heavily engaged with a Viet Cong battalion. Al had the Peter Pilot, who was a W-1—

"wobbly-one," or warrant officer one—warm up the big bird. They lifted off and headed for the wounded man and the FO.

Al took a long look at the situation while they approached, and he didn't like what he saw. The ARVN battalion had apparently withdrawn into light jungle for about two hundred meters. The two American advisers had been left under heavy fire. They were out in the paddies taking refuge behind a dike. The VC battalion was in another patch of light jungle about a hundred meters east of the pinned-down Americans.

An Air Force FAC in an O-1 flew in lazy circles, while two F-4A Phantom jets screamed down out of the heavens and pounded the Viet Cong positions with five-hundred-pound explosive eggs and napalm. Al watched two napalm canisters drop from a streaking bird that passed across the jungle, missed, and exploded across the paddies, their flaming jel burning on the ground, right up to the edge of the position where the two Americans were ducking.

Al called the FAC and asked it to stop the air strike so he could pick up the wounded American RTO.

The bird dog replied, "Dust-off, my boys still have a little ordnance. Let them soften Charlie up a little more, and we'll get out of your way. Over."

"Negative," Al Nichols replied firmly. "I got Americans to pick up, and I'm going in now. If you boys are set on blowing people up, you'll just have to lay your eggs on me, out."

With that, Al reached down with his right hand and pushed down on the cyclic, which changed the tilt of the giant rotor overhead. Reaching down with his left hand, he pulled on the collective, grabbing air, pushed down on his left pedal, and headed his medevac in a beeline toward the wounded soldier and the FO. Teeth gritted, he decided he had a mission to accomplish, and he was going to do it.

The FAC called the jets off immediately, and they went back on-station, somewhere out of sight up in the cloud-filled blue skies.

Al had the flashing red light on top of his chopper going when he went in to pick up the Americans. That flashing light seemed to become a target as numerous bullets hit all around it and whizzed by it. As Al approached the two men in the chopper, he could see scorched ground and some flames right up to their position.

Bullets crashing all around, the FO—an old gray-haired sergeant—stood up and waved Al off. Just then, a bullet crashed into Al's light, and red plastic pieces flew all over the place. Trying to wave Al off, the sergeant waved his arms back and forth frantically, and Al pulled up on the cyclic.

The sight that Al saw before he pulled up would remain in his mind from then on. The ballsy gray-haired NCO stood there waving the chopper off, exposing himself to intense enemy fire, bullets kicking up in the water and mud all around him and between his legs. Nevertheless, the sergeant stood there braving the fire to keep Al from getting shot to pieces.

As usual in a tight situation, Al climbed up doing zigzags until he reached about seventy to eighty knots, then he pulled the collective up, changing the blades' angle, and climbed rapidly at about a thousand feet per minute until he was out of gunshot range. He headed back toward Dong Team to refuel as quickly as possible.

Al was back within thirty minutes, escorted by two Huey gunships from the Vikings. His mind was made up; he would land this time, no matter what. The American

RTO, he had learned, was shot through both thighs and had to get to a hospital.

"Viking Five-Niner," Al transmitted, "bullets are thicker'n shit down there, and I gotta have cover. Can you help me out? Over."

"Rog-O," came the reply. "Stand back a minute."

The two armed Hueys flew over the battle zone and dropped several big smoke canisters between the Americans and the VC positions. In seconds, smoke belched out of the Jolly Green Giant smoke grenades. The two gunboats started pouring ordnance on the bad guys, and Al dropped down to the deck. He poured the coals to his airborne ambulance and brought it in full speed, its skids almost touching the ground. Even though the gunships were firing, the VC still fired at Al, trying their best to knock him out of the air.

He made it to the position of the two Americans and set down on the paddy dike. In the meantime the two gunships up above started swirling around, banking their choppers in such a manner that they were almost completely sideways. The door gunners of each gunship fired straight down with their M-60 machine guns, creating a deadly but protective veil of 7.62-millimeter bullets around the medevac helicopter.

Al's medic and crew chief jumped out of the chopper and dashed through the withering fire to grab the wounded RTO. Again exposing himself to enemy fire, the gray-haired NCO stood up to help lift the wounded man into their arms. They dashed to the chopper, and he turned and resumed firing at the nearby enemy forces.

Al opened his door and hopped out, yelling at the NCO, "Come on! Come on, Sergeant!"

The man waved him off and yelled back, "I ain't wounded, sir! Get the fuck outta here!"

Al yelled, "I don't care if you're wounded, I'm not leaving you!"

The man waved a quick thank-you gesture and hollered, "This is my job, sir! I got it to do, and you got yours! Get your ass the fuck out of here, and save my man!"

Al hopped into the bird and gave the man a wave. The man nodded, grinned, and winked at Al, then whirled around firing at the VC. Al cranked on the cyclic and collective and got the hell out of Dodge.

He hadn't put his helmet on yet when he heard agonized yelling from the back of the aircraft. He looked back, and his medic gave him a glance and laugh. The medic was shooting a morphine syrette into the wounded man's butt. Normally he would shoot it into the side of the thigh, but the poor RTO had bullet holes through both of them. The man kept yelling something with tears in his eyes, and Al assumed he was hysterical over getting shot. He asked the medic about it.

Using the helmet mike, the medic answered, "Hell no, sir. This poor guy keeps apologizing over and over again because he shit his pants. The last napalm burned right up to the edge of their position."

Al and his wobbly-one laughed heartily as they fought the controls and the demons that wanted to hold the chopper back and catch a few bullets. Al called the CO of the Vikings and told him about the gray-haired forward observer down below and asked if they would supply the man with air cover. He was too fucking brave to get killed on account of a chickenshit ARVN battalion that had deserted him and left him exposed in the middle of the open paddies while they took refuge in the jungle.

Al finally made it back to the base camp near Dong Team, dropped the wounded man off, refueled, and headed back to the base camp.

Landing there, he checked on the FO and found that the brave old noncom had rejoined the ARVN unit after numerous air strikes had routed the VC.

Al sat in the chopper on the tarmac, and the Viking commander's slick helicopter landed next to him. The crew chief hopped out and ran over to Al.

"Captain," the crew chief said, "the old man wants your name and the names of all your crew members."

Al gave him a funny look. "What's wrong? Did we fuck up?"

The crew chief laughed. "Fuck no, sir. The boss is putting you and your crew in for medals."

Al replied, "That's great, but please make sure my crew chief and medic get Silver Stars. They earned it. They—"

"He heard about it from the gunships, sir," the crew chief said. "He is putting them in for Silvers, and you and your Peter Pilot are getting the DFC."

Al smiled. "The Distinguished Flying Cross, huh? That's really nice. Tell the major I said thanks a lot."

A couple of weeks had passed, and Al was feeling restless, and useless. A monsoon had blown in off the South China Sea and was playing hell with the weather in the Mekong Delta region, as well as with the emotions of the American soldiers.

This particular day wasn't rainy. It was just foggy all day and into the evening. Al couldn't take his chopper up simply because he wasn't allowed to. His job was to fly into the jaws of death and save people's lives, day and night. Sitting around drinking Ba Muoi Ba, the Vietnamese beer, or "33," or the Filipino beer San Miguel, was just not what Al wanted to do all day.

Night came, and Al Nichols found himself in a game

of High Chicago with other chopper pilots. He had the ace of spades and two pair, so he bumped the pot five bucks, hoping that wasn't so high a raise that it would scare everyone out of the game. It wasn't. As he hoped, the CW3 across from him, who had been raising, raised another five, and the rest called. Nobody folded yet.

Al called, and cards were asked for. The guy who opened took three, the one who raised stood pat, and the other two took one card. Al stood pat. He figured the others for four cards to a flush or straight, or possibly two pair. Al assumed that the one who stood pat had either a flush or a straight, or two pair and the king of spades. In High Chicago, the highest spade played splits the pot with the best poker hand.

Al had the ace of spades already, so he would bump like hell because he couldn't lose. The guy who opened checked to the first raiser, and the chief warrant bet twenty dollars. The guy next to him folded, and Al called and bumped him twenty more. The guy next to him hesitated too long, but he called. The man who opened showed his openers—a pair of queens—and folded. Pretty soon it was just Al, the chief, and the guy next to Al.

The chief bumped fifty dollars, and Al called, as there was a three-raise limit on the table stakes game. The man to Al's left called, and the chief warrant's face flushed. He grinned at Al.

"You're called, chief," Al said. "Show your fucking hand."

The man laid the cards down. He had a pair of tens, not even enough to have opened. He had simply been bluffing.

Al said, "Man, you aren't going to buy a pot in a game like High Chicago. Somebody will always have a high spade."

The man didn't speak. He was too embarrassed.

The guy next to Al, a lieutenant, said, "No shit," and he plopped down the king of spades and two pair, sevens and treys.

Al grinned, took a swallow of San Miguel, and said, "Yeah, no shit."

He flopped down his hand and showed his two pair—eights and treys—and the ace of spades.

"I'll be fucked," the first lieutenant by Al said.

"You are," Al replied as he raked the pot in.

Al's crew chief stuck his head in the door and said to Al, "Sir, the old man wants to see anyone who wants to get killed."

Al and the lieutenant he had just defeated, along with the chief warrant, all jumped up and left the room. They went to the TOC, and found a major standing in front of a briefing map. He had a blue grease pencil in his right hand, and he pointed to a squad-size symbol in the Seven Mountains area. The three men stood around the map, along with four gunship pilots.

The major spoke. "This is classified top secret, by the way. You guys know the rules. There is a nine-man unit, all wounded, that has been socked in right here in the Seven Mountains area. They were on a top secret mission in Cambodia. All are wearing sterilized uniforms. Three of them are Americans, and one of them is near death. Two of the indigenous are critical as well. They have to get medical attention, but the whole area has been socked in as thick as it is here. I need a volunteer."

Al headed toward the door. "I got to get my bird warmed up, sir," he said.

The lieutenant followed Al out the door saying, "Major, I'll take care of Captain Nichols's ass, there and back."

The other pilots kind of shuffled their feet nervously.

When Al arrived at his dust-off, a big grin spread over his face. The chopper was already warming up on the tarmac, his crew all in place. As he approached his door, the wobbly-one greeted him and handed him his white-painted helmet.

The warrant said, "We figured you'd get us out of this boring place somehow, sir. Wherever we need to go, we're ready."

Al put on his helmet and spoke into the mike, "Listen, you guys. This is a heavy-duty mission, and you need to—"

The crew chief interrupted him with his hand up, while checking the outside of the chopper. "Captain, this is obviously a dangerous mission we're going on. We better not waste time talking."

The other men looked at Al, both grinning. He grinned back, and they checked communications with the other dust-off that was going to follow Al.

Al looked over at Peter Pilot and said, "This fucking DECE system better work good, or we will become land-scape."

The other chopper started warming up, so Al had his crew chief go back through his preflight checks again. He believed that could never be done enough. Minutes later, the medevac helicopter lifted off, followed by the first lieutenant in the other one. He told Al that he would have to keep from getting his red light shot off again, because he would be keying on that to fly.

Al said over the radio, "If you are going to watch my light, you better stay awful close to me. Over."

The lieutenant's laughing voice came back over the radio. "Close? Dust-off Eight-Five, I hope you got a jar of Vaseline. Over."

"Not quite that close. Out." Al laughed into his own mike.

The DECE system utilized three sending and receiving stations. There was a little roll map in the cockpit and a pointer sticking down from the center of the device that held the map, which rolled back and forth. The helicopter sent a signal out that was picked up by three different stations. The stations would shoot an azimuth on the radio signal and constantly triangulate the exact spot where Al's chopper was. This was transmitted to the inboard computer in his chopper, which pointed on the map exactly where the helicopter was. The map rolled backward or forward as the pointer did.

Al set a heading for the Seven Mountains region and put the pedal to the metal. The louey behind him had no trouble following, as he stayed right on Nichols's ass.

In too quick a time to suit anyone, the real test came. They arrived at the Seven Mountains region. Al looked down at the DECE map and saw mountains looming straight ahead. He would have to enter through a pass going south, then turning west. He looked out his bubble and saw nothing but swirling gray with a faint tint of flashing red from his top light.

His eyes went back to the map, and he rubbed them as they teared up from strain. Nobody was jabbering over the intercom, as the crew sometimes did. There wasn't even any of the nervous joking that went on going into hot LZs. All eyes stared out into the gray shroud enveloping them within the bigger shroud of blackness, which was moonless night.

Al calculated that they were passing between the two tall mountains, and he tilted the cyclic to move south. His big hands moved the cyclic ever so slightly to make the powerful craft turn, dive, rise, or whatever. That was one of the big keys to driving those machines effectively—subtle movements of the hand, not exaggerated ones.

Al now had a bigger challenge. According to the map, a giant mountain was looming in front of him and others on each side. He would have to turn slightly north to keep from ramming into the mountainside, then turn back west again as he went around it through a narrow canyon. Al pushed forward, sweat running down his forehead and into his eyes, his gaze affixed to the little moving map in the center of the instrument panel.

Down below, a U.S. Special Forces lieutenant and two staff sergeants lay on the ground with six Chinese Nung mercenaries. None of the men had any patches or "Made in the USA" identification on their person, weapons, or equipment. They lay on the ground with the ranking man, the young officer smoking a cigarette. He passed it to one of the sergeants, who took several drags and passed it on to the other sergeant. The men hid their worried thoughts from each other and calmly smoked the Camel.

The lieutenant finally broke the silence. "Well, at least Charlie's going to have a fuckin' hard time finding us in this thick shit."

The second sergeant said, "Yeah, *Trung-uy,* but nobody else will find us, either. Looks like we're dead motherfuckers."

The other sergeant said quietly, "There's a dust-off on the way right now."

Both men stared at him, then looked at each other. The sergeant was a Mescalero Apache who had grown up in Arizona and New Mexico. He never spoke much, except with the Swedish K and Barnett crossbow and bolts he carried on every operation.

In the distance they heard the echoing sound of helicopter rotor blades coming toward them.

Both soldiers stared at each other again and shook

their heads. "How the fuck did you know that a chopper was coming?" the lieutenant asked the sergeant.

The Apache sergeant looked at the ash on the end of the cigarette and spoke softly. "Because I knew it was coming."

The two stared at each other again and shrugged their shoulders.

"I don't understand," the white sergeant said.

"You should," the Apache said. "You both should."

"Why?" the lieutenant asked.

"Because, like me, you are warriors."

"Sergeant," the officer came back as the sounds of Al's chopper got closer, "what in the fuck are you talking up?"

"Yeah, man?" the other said.

The Apache said, "Have you ever been standing there, and all of a sudden you turn around because you know somebody is looking at your back?"

The two nodded, simultaneously saying, "Yeah, I have."

The Apache lit another cigarette, cupping the hot ember in his right hand, and took a long drag. He held the cigarette up and offered it to each of the four compass points. He took another drag and slowly inhaled, then blew out a long puff of smoke.

"What are you doing now, Sarge?" the lieutenant asked.

He smiled. "Smoking a cigarette, sir."

Al Nichols called them on the radio, and the white sergeant keyed his mike twice, not really wanting to break radio silence. The men had infiltrated into Cambodia by CH-34 chopper, then headed east back toward Vietnam on foot. They had located an NVA regimental staging area and crept in during the night to booby-trap some of the

NVA ammunition. Their job was reconnaissance, but the direct action mission would be an added bonus.

While the rest of the team formed a perimeter of safety, the Apache sergeant and the young officer had crept into a cache of 7.62-millimeter ammunition and taken several bullets apart, pouring out the gunpowder. They replaced the gunpowder with Composition C-4 plastic explosive, then put the bullets back together and replaced them in the bunker, which was partially hidden at that point.

Later on, some unlucky NVA soldier would aim his AK-47, his SKS rifle, or a machine gun at an American and fire. The weapon would explode in his face, killing him and causing future soldiers in the unit to be a little more tentative in their aiming of weapons. Maybe it would save some American lives, and maybe it wouldn't, but it was definitely worth the risk in the minds of these professional warriors.

After they sabotaged the ammo, they started to exfiltrate the regimental headquarters area, mostly snaking along the ground on their bellies. They stopped at one point nearby, and the Apache crawled into a small stand of bamboo and placed a small beeper homing device in some boxes of supplies hidden there. They reasoned that the boxes would be moved with the regiment since they were not buried. If the NVA moved into a new area, the boxes would probably go with them, along with the homing device, if it had not been discovered.

American pilots in Mohawk aircraft would fly near the border and pick up a continuous radio beeping signal from the device. They would shoot two directional azimuths on it, pinpointing the precise location of the beeper at the apex of the two azimuths. Until the beeper was discovered, U.S. military intelligence could keep track of the NVA regiment and determine its size as well, along with their normal job of monitoring radio conversations and the strength of the signals.

The RT succeeded in the mission, but on their way back to a preplanned extraction point about five klicks away from the regimental staging area, they ran into an incoming NVA company that was returning from a cross-border excursion into Vietnam.

At that point the familiar brown excretive material really hit the fan. The Chinese Nungs fought like tigers, much to the joy of the Americans, who equaled them in ferocity. The NVA unit kept splitting off into squad-size units, trying to block the retreat of the Americans. Finally the SOG personnel, shot to doll-rags, assembled literally back to back in a stand of bamboo.

They all touched hands, and with an SF statement of "Fuck it!" they decided to charge right down the dirt road they had been traveling and try to break through the NVA's strongest elements—their least expected escape route.

They did it. Somehow, fighting and firing, picking out targets of opportunity, they broke through and made flight for the border, running into the gravy-thick fog a mile later. After that, it was fairly easy to get away, but their hopes were fading as the lifeblood of most of them seeped into the wet Cambodian, then South Vietnamese soil. Picking a spot easy to defend, they decided to make their stand in the Seven Mountains.

That was where Al Nichols, followed by the other dust-off, made his heroic DECE-guided flight. He came down to the silent cheers and the weak but broad smiles of the courageous warriors.

The entire team survived the flight to the hospital in the two airborne ambulances. Back in the "world," nobody would hear about them or their actions, or Al Nichols and his crew on the evening news. Instead, viewers would be treated to a nightly dose of students protesting and burning draft cards and the American flag, mixed in with a few shots of American GIs setting fire to Vietnamese hamlets, while VC-sympathizing old men and old women squatted in front of the cameras and cried their eyes out.

The next day, lying in his room, Al felt as if every muscle in his body ached. He apparently had been so tense flying out to save the wounded that he now hurt as if he had run against the world's best racehorses in the Kentucky Derby. He reached over for the cup of coffee next to his bed, and a moan escaped his lips. He took a drink of the scalding brew, as he sat up, legs dangling over the edge of the bed. He set the coffee down and lay back on the bed to let his body and nerves recuperate some more.

Folding his hands behind his head, the young captain thought back to another long, tiring operation that he had gotten one of his medals for.

It was during the previous year, December 9, 1967, in fact. Al had been flying direct support for a combined South Vietnamese and American airmobile operation, along with mechanized infantry support. The area of operations was north of Vi Thanh in Chuong Thien province, about twenty-seven miles southwest of Can Tho and smack in the middle of the Mekong Delta region.

A company of the Ninth Infantry Division was acting as a blocking element for an ARVN company that was sweeping along a series of rice paddies and dikes, with occasional patches of light jungle here and there in the table-flat tactical area of operations. To the south of this unit was a mechanized infantry unit from the South Vietnamese Army, which acted as an additional sweeping force as well as a flank for the ARVN straight-legs.

A platoon from ARVN company got ambushed not long after daybreak. They had been sweeping across a small rice paddy, moving almost on line, as they went from one patch of jungle to another, a half-mile distant. As they approached one paddy dike, a soldier who had been moving in front as part of a close point patrol suddenly screamed out in pain. The two men next to him grabbed him and dragged him to one of the dikes along the side of the paddy. A razor-sharp bamboo punji stake was sticking through his left leg. The stake had entered the front of the leg through the shin and projected upward, exiting the leg at the top of the calf. Human feces were smeared all over it, an additional VC trick to add some infection or gangrene to the wound, just for effect.

The man who walked into the punji stake had been on the right side of the paddy, so the platoon leader shifted the entire platoon a little to the left, while a medic and a rifleman attended to the wounded soldier. This was just what Charlie wanted.

Just as the unit reached the end of paddy and was about to climb out and cross over the long dike, the camouflaged lids of numerous spiderholes flew up off the top the dike. Suddenly, the heads and shoulders of a score of Viet Cong soldiers appeared, pointing deadly AK-47s and several machine guns at the platoon of South Vietnamese soldiers. The deadly point-blank ambush opened up, and the entire front line of the ARVN fell under the Communist fusillade.

In a panic, the balance of the platoon turned and ran back the way they had come, the platoon leader at the front, his eyes wide in panic. Only the platoon sergeant, a professional soldier with many battles under his belt, tried to halt the complete rout of his men, but his efforts were in vain.

He finally did get them stopped behind the next dike, where they hugged the ground for cover. Some of the braver ones soon appeared over the top of the dike, helping wounded comrades out of the rice paddy. The first wounded man over the dike, though, was met with a deadly burst of fire from a young ARVN soldier's M-16 rifle. The soldier had dropped his cousin, who he was helping back, because he was sporting a sucking chest wound from the initial ambush.

Neither of these men would ever go home to work his father's rice paddy.

The platoon sergeant immediately called for a medevac and asked his MAC-V American adviser for an air traffic controller. The adviser ended up calling and directing the air strike on the VC position. The Commies, however, simply ducked down into their spiderholes and fired at the enemy, while the jets pulled out of their dives.

Al Nichols had already been airborne in a standby mode when he got the order to pick up wounded from the ARVN unit. The jets had dropped their ordnance and bugged by the time Al arrived in his dust-off. Another pair of fast-movers would not be on station for ten minutes yet.

Captain Nichols leaned that powerful rotor forward and grabbed all the thick, wet air he could. The big bird zipped toward the firefight. Al came in low-leveling over the shimmering paddies and little green strips of paddy dikes that crisscrossed the landscape and made it all look from the air like a giant green, brown, and blue checkerboard. The VC were now pouring small-arms and automatic-weapons fire onto the ducking ARVN soldiers.

Al Nichols became their new target as soon as they saw the big olive-drab chopper approaching with the easy target on its side—a giant white circle with a red cross in the middle.

With intense enemy fire hitting the chopper and cracking all around it, Al brought the craft in. He stopped at a hover just over the paddy water's surface. Several of the braver ARVN soldiers, after an order from the now-composed platoon leader, tossed out the smoke for Al.

Al held the dust-off there, totally exposed to the deadly hail of bullets, until the five ARVN soldiers had been lifted or tossed onboard.

Crack-crack-crack-crack!   Whump-whump-whump-whump!

A quick burst of automatic-weapons fire actually went through one open door of the Huey and out the other door, just missing everyone by scant inches but miraculously hitting nothing.

Al grabbed the cyclic in one hand and the collective in the other and was about to do his thing when he saw movement in the tall grass in front of the chopper. With bullets tearing into the skin of the ship and cracking through the air all around, he nosed the craft forward. Then he saw an American soldier, an adviser from MAC-V, was lying on the ground and trying to crawl toward the dust-off.

The bones were sticking out from the top and bottom of the man's right knee, which had simply been shot off. Another bullet had gone through his left hip, and the exit hole had taken part of his buttocks cheek with it. Captain Nichols inched the chopper forward through the hail of withering fire and brought it to a hover, the skid within a foot or two of the wounded American's arm. The medic and crew chief jumped out while Al fired an M-16 out the door in support of them. The enemy were just a series of blinking lights and flashes in the far treeline, but each one of those flashes carried a message of instant death and destruction. Victor Charlie was trying to communicate that message as rapidly as possible.

The two men got the wounded American aboard. Al grabbed the controls firmly, then cranked it and took off in his ordinary zigzag maneuver, climbing until he was out of bullet range. He then nosed the Huey toward the far-off ARVN hospital and floored that baby, going through the gears.

Several hours later, the crew had finished refueling and making quick patch jobs on the chopper. It was well past dark at that time, when Al was told to go back to the same area to pick up thirteen badly wounded ARVN soldiers. This time, they were from the mechanized infantry unit.

Al flew out across a silent plain, knowing that down below thousands of pairs of eyes belonging to enemy soldiers were staring up at the steel bird, watching from all over the ground, horizon to horizon. Al wondered how many of those eyes were looking across the sights of a gun.

He gritted his teeth tightly and reached up to his forehead to wipe several gallons of perspiration away. Officers perspired; enlisted men sweated. He shook the cobwebs clear from his mind and listened to the rhythmic drums coming from the folds of his empty stomach.

The firefight was still far off on the horizon, but the sight kept getting closer and closer. Numerous tracers sent laserlike lines across the skies in various directions. Every once in a while, flashes appeared from explosions.

As Al approached the firefight, some of those tracers suddenly streaked at him and his aircraft. There was an American adviser with the ARVN, and Al called him on the radio to ask him to mark his position. The adviser said he didn't know how. Al couldn't believe it.

"What do you mean, you don't know how? Over," Al said.

The adviser answered, "We used up all our parachute flares trying to spot Charlie sneaking up. Over."

"How about your headlights? Over."

"They shot them out. Over."

Al said, "I have no flares. Make a circle for me, and just have on your running lights. Over."

"Wilco," the man answered. "But some of the running lights are knocked out, too. Over."

Al said quickly, "Use a flashlight. Point it straight up. Over."

"Wilco. Out" came the reply.

A burst of automatic-weapons fire tore through the back part of Al's fuselage. The crew chief called him on the intercom and told him there was no damage. Al banked the chopper and swung out wide over the valley.

Al automatically looked at the DECE system to make sure there were no mountains in the vicinity. He knew there weren't, but he checked anyway. The night, again, was moonless, but the ground, as usual, looked lighter from the air than it would from the ground.

Al made a wide swing out over the valley and looked at the ARVN unit's location. The fire from the enemy positions seemed to increase. Al lifted a pair of binoculars to his eyes and looked out the front of his chopper. He couldn't see a thing and took the glasses down. Laughing at himself, he realized he had been looking at his own windshield-wiper blade and arm. He looked again and saw the APC finally moving into place around the makeshift LZ.

Al turned out his lights and went down to the deck.

Keying his mike, he said, "Be ready. Coming in low, lights out. Over."

"Roger. Out."

Captain Nichols was several feet off the surface of the

paddies, after turning out his lights and banking the bird. He pushed the cyclic forward and angled the blades radically with the collective. The dust-off zoomed across the countryside toward the hellfires ahead.

Into the jaws of death, black death, Al pushed his craft. He flew into the circle of tiny lights made by the armored personnel carriers and quickly pulled into a hover, with the tail back, his rear skids touching the ground. He set the chopper down and watched the seeming thousands of tiny lights blinking as enemy soldiers tried their best to kill him, his men, and his machine. Every once in a while, the sources of the little flashes would spew forth a deadly tracer that flew past the helicopter and its whirring blades.

Al kept glancing back nervously as one, two, three, four, and finally, five wounded South Vietnamese soldiers were somehow crammed onboard his airborne ambulance. Al waved at the American adviser standing off to the side of the chopper and took off straight at the blinking lights, his light beam in their eyes. He knew that if he could zoom right at and over them, it would probably take them by surprise and keep their heads down.

He was weary and sore and dead tired, but he had to get out of another tough situation. Bullets were hitting all around the chopper, with a few more glancing off or tearing the skins here and there.

It was well into night. He had made two trips now to pick up wounded. As the last of the fuel was poured into the big thirsty bird, Al gulped: a call came in for him to pick up more wounded at the site.

Not wanting to demoralize his crew as deeply as he was, he feigned happiness. "Great news, guys. We did such a great job picking up the wounded, they want us to go back and pick up some more."

Al saw a dejected look come over every crew member's face. "Saddle up," he said firmly. "There's people out there dying, praying we'll come to save them."

This seemed to snap all the men out of it, and they hurried to get ready to go back out into the unforgiving tracer-filled skies.

Twenty minutes later, Al saw that the fighting had started again with renewed vigor. He didn't know if air strikes or indirect-fire weapons had been employed, but he wondered why the bad guys were still there, still shooting. It didn't matter. He had to take his dust-off in again and pick up the frightened young VN who were wounded.

This time, Al made his approach straight in, no messing around. He didn't care who shot at him or how many times. He was going straight in and straight out again, and he was going to pick up any and all wounded, period.

He came to a hover, and the ARVN started carrying wounded men on expedient litters and placing them onboard. Within seconds, with bullets still creasing the air about them, the dust-off crew had eleven more wounded onboard. Al cranked up the big bird, then glanced over and saw two blindfolded Viet Cong prisoners, their hands tied. Both were bleeding from wounds near their shoulders.

The American adviser was not in sight, so Al used sign language to tell a Vietnamese *thieu-uy,* or second lieutenant, to load the prisoners onboard. The man shrugged and had several soldiers shove the two VC on board. With his thirteen new charges onboard moaning in pain, Nichols took off straight ahead then zoomed into a banking climb. He zigzagged back and forth until he reached eighty knots, then climbed toward Heaven, trying to put as much atmosphere between the hooligans and his aircraft as possible.

* * *

Al lay back on his cot and shook his head as he thought back to that night. He had been in the air for twelve hours straight, with his adrenaline pumping and all his senses on full alert. The emotional strain was what was so damned tiring. A very tired Captain Nichols closed his eyes and wondered what lay ahead for him.

"Dust-off Eight-Five, this is Texas Smoke Two-Niner, over" came the voice crackling over the radio.

Al looked out the bubble of his Huey. "Go ahead, Two-Niner. You got Dust-off Eight-Five. Over."

"Eight-Five, Two-Niner, we have been pinned down by sniper fire. We can't cut an LZ, and we have three wounded to get out of here. Over."

Al replied, "We're on our way. Be there in five minutes. Hang tough. Over."

Al was pilot on this mission, and he looked at the aircraft commander. Both men raised their eyebrows and pursed their lips, simultaneously blowing out deep sighs. Another hot mission, another hot LZ. Would it ever end?

It was February 4, 1968, and Al didn't know, nor did anyone know, that a few weeks later, he would be busier than ever. The Chinese New Year, Tet, would be celebrated throughout Vietnam, and the North Vietnamese and Viet Cong would launch a major coordinated offensive in conjunction with the annual nationwide celebration.

They approached the area where the operation was pinned down. It was a large patch of jungle surrounded by numerous paddies and dikes. The wounded were soldiers of the Ninth Infantry Division.

Al said, "Two-Niner, pop us smoke. Over."

Seconds later, the two pilots saw some green smoke lazily swirling up through the trees.

Al said, "I see green. Over."

"That's us," came the reply.

The Alpha Charlie nodded at Al to bring the chopper down in a tight circle toward the tiny clearing where the smoke was. Al spotted some more green smoke swirling up through the trees about seventy-five meters from the first spot. He pulled the chopper back up and started climbing.

"Two-Niner, this is Dust-off Eight-Five. I see two green smokes now. How many did you pop? Over."

"Just one" came the reply. "They must be watching and copying our smoke. Over."

Al said, "You got a pyro? Over."

"Roger. Over."

Al said, "When I request the end of your lit stogie, send that along with the pyro. Over."

"Wilco, out!" came the quick reply.

Al started back down and keyed his mike a minute later. "Two-Niner, give us a smoke. Over."

He soon saw yellow smoke swirling up through the trees, followed seconds later by yellow smoke swirling up from the other position. Then a little streak shot up into the sky from the first position, and a hand-held parachute flare popped open in front of Al's chopper and started its lazy descent toward the light canopy of the jungle. The AC winked at Al, and the big captain laughed as he headed the dust-off at the location of the first smoke.

The chopper was one minute away from setting down when withering automatic-weapons fire suddenly started pouring out of the VC position. The chopper had to bank sharply right and crank away as quickly as possible. They circled, and when they started back down toward the LZ, the automatic-weapons fire started up again, as well as additional ground fire from numerous NVA guns.

"Eight-Five, Eight-Five, stay away. We got ground troops on the way for help. Hold off a little. It's too dangerous. Over," came the voice from the ground commander.

"Roger, standing by. Out," Al replied.

A half hour later, Al got the call that the LZ was secured and the VC troops had been pushed back from the area. They made the approach with the thought that the dust-off would land this time, no matter what. The wounds that the three Americans had suffered were too grave.

They again asked for smoke, and this time only the one that the Americans popped swirled lazily up through the canopy. It was purple smoke, and it swirled back down into the trees as the helicopter passed overhead. Following that, little jets of purple smoke shot out from under branches all around the outside of the rotor blast.

Al could see expressions of relief on the faces of the wounded men, lying down below on expedient poncho stretchers. Suddenly, out of the stillness, automatic-weapons fire snapped and cracked again, whizzing by the chopper crew's heads and ears. They didn't care. They had a mission to accomplish. The rifle company on the ground opened up in every direction, and Al called the position of the sniper to the ground commander.

The firing stopped as the big bird dropped below the tops of the trees. The skids touched the ground, and the three men were placed onboard, to be cared for by the dust-off medic. The chopper pulled straight up in a hover and immediately drew the automatic-weapons fire again. Al almost laid the chopper on its side as he banked sharply away from the sniper's position.

Dust-off 85 sped away from the twisting, spinning, high-velocity shards of death and headed for the relative safety of a foreign town, filled with enemies who posed as friends and hid behind friendly smiles.

* * *

July 13, 1968, found Captain Al Nichols a little bit older, a little bit wiser, a little bit more experienced, and a lot more worn out. No matter what, though, he was a medical evacuation pilot, and he could not help himself. His job was to extract wounded soldiers from battlefields. Hopefully that could be done without getting shot at, but on occasion, bullets would be trying to clip his ears and ventilate his system. Still, he could not and would not try to get out of flying out on a mission. Al just felt that such a thing wouldn't be right.

Al and his crew were on support that day, for the ARVN and regional forces in the area of operations. A call came in that three ARVN soldiers were gravely wounded on the top of Nui Kto Mountain. Another medevac had tried to make an extraction several times but had had to withdraw because of enemy sniper fire.

One of the ARVN troops had a sucking chest wound, and bubbling frothy blood was coming out of the exit wound. Another had been shot through the left shoulder and the right calf. The third had had his eye taken out by an AK bullet that had passed across his face at an angle.

While approaching Nui Kto, Al put his medic on the horn with a Vietnamese *trung-si,* or sergeant, who was with the unit and had previously worked as an interpreter. The medic asked about the man with the sucking chest wound and was told that they had put an Army bandage on it, but the man was sinking fast.

The medic told the Vietnamese sergeant to have the medic take the plastic wrapper from the Army bandage and place it over the bullet hole, then tape the edges so there would be an airtight seal over the wound. The VN didn't understand, so the medic explained that the bullet had penetrated one of the man's lungs and the hole had to be covered, so the air wouldn't escape.

Five minutes later, the Vietnamese interpreter reported that the soldier was bandaged properly, lying on his side, and was doing much better. The medic told him to bandage both eyes of the man who had lost one to keep the good eye still and to keep from doing more damage inside the other eye socket, and stand by. The VN reported that the one with the shoulder and leg wound was laughing and joking and smoking a cigarette. The medic told him that was fine, but he had to lie down with his feet elevated and a poncho liner over him to prevent him from going into shock.

Al had to fly low to the location because of the very low ceiling—it was hanging only about a hundred feet over Nui Kto. As he approached the jungle-covered mountaintop, a gunship circling nearby warned him away.

Just as he started to make his turn, two sets of tracers poured off the slopes of the steep ridge and chased after his banking aircraft like a pair of hungry coyotes pursuing a frightened snowshoe hare.

"Dust-off Eight-Five, this is Viking Two-Three. Over" came the call from the command gunship.

"Go ahead, Two-Three," Al replied.

"Roger, Eight-Five. There's a number of hooligans down there on both sides of the slopes, and they got telescopes on their popguns. Over."

"Good read on that," Al said. "You just keep on eye on the front, back, and side doors, and I'll do a little Santa Claus number with the chimney. Over."

"Viking Two-Three here. Rog-O. You go to your hiding place, and I'll make Charlie hide his eyes while you're hiding. Over."

"This is a fun game already. Do your thing, Two-Three. I'm doing mine right now. Out," Al replied.

Al looked back and saw an armed Huey swing around

one side of the mountain and the other gunboat swing around the other. Suddenly, rockets spewed from the nostrils of the gunships, followed by 7.62-millimeter machine-gun fire. As usual, every fifth round was a tracer. The tracers made wavy arcs as they sped toward the mountainside and disappeared into the morass of brilliant green colors.

Confident that most of the NVA would now be hiding their heads in the sand, Al grabbed the controls and cranked that chopper toward Venus. He disappeared into the thick clouds, and there was soon a *pop-pop-pop* sound somewhere up there in the white gravy. Looking at his DECE and radar screens, Al headed back toward the mountaintop and started circling downward.

"This is Dust-off Eight-Five again," he said to the ground commander. "You have your buddies ready to be loaded onboard when you see me. Pop a smoke."

A voice with a thick Vietnamese accent crackled back over the radio, "Roger, but I no see you. Over."

Al said, "Don't worry about that. I'll be there. Out."

The Vietnamese commander tossed out a smoke grenade on the bare mountaintop, and seconds later, Al Nichols's chopper dropped straight down out of the cloud cover and descended on the smoke grenade. As he got right down to the deck, the rotor wash sent clouds of yellow smoke down against and along the ground, then upward twenty feet beyond the reach of the giant blades.

Al felt and heard bullets rip into the skin of the aircraft even before the skids hit the ground. He looked over and saw several blinking flashes in the dark shadows of the nearby jungle. Giving the Peter Pilot a grim look, he got the hell out of Dodge, again taking the chopper into an almost vertical climb into the relative safety of the dense cloud cover.

Al streaked away from the mountain and made a fast

turn, headed back at top speed, and pulled into a hover directly above where he thought the mountaintop was. He dropped down and down and was soon below the thick white billows of moisture. He was indeed directly above the mountaintop.

Al dropped down thirty feet more and held his hover at about seventy feet above the mountain. He directed the crew chief to drop the basket with the hoist; then Al looked down below and saw tracers streaking at his helicopter from the jungle again. He also saw ARVN soldiers firing back.

When the pilot gave him a weird look, Al said, "When we were on the deck, they had a clean shot at us, but I think they'll have trouble reaching us through the jungle canopy if we stay up here."

Just then, a bullet ripped through the armor and passed between Al and the pilot, ricocheting off the frame of Al's seat, then spending itself in Al's war bag, tucked away under the pilot's seat.

Al grinned at the pilot and raised his eyebrows. "So much for my fucking theories and tactics. Guess our job's always going to be dangerous."

The pilot was frightened, but Al's joking made him laugh. The young warrant officer relaxed a little as the basket made the ground and two Vietnamese were placed in it at the same time. The aircraft hovered like a sitting duck while snipers fired at the ascending ARVN wounded. When the basket reached the craft, the crew chief, standing on the skid, snatched it and swung it onboard. Then the basket was dropped again, and another sniper round tore into the helicopter's flesh.

Al refused to pull out. The empty basket reached the ground, and the soldier with the sucking chest wound was strapped into it. The crew chief pushed the button and winched the wounded man skyward. Through the Plexiglas bubble in front of his feet, Al saw a gunship pass below him, barely missing his hoist cable. The craft swung quickly, and the Alpha Charlie laid the craft almost up on his side.

Al got a lump in his throat for some reason as the door gunner on the gunship stood on the skid with both feet, a safety cable holding him in space like a metal tether or man-made umbilical cord. The door gunner poured deadly machine-gun fire at the snipers' positions while the gunship stayed close to Al, between Al and the snipers.

Al said quickly, "Thanks, partner."

A voice came back on the radio: "Hey, slick pilots and gunboat pilots might not get along, but everyone loves dust-offs, man."

Five minutes passed, and the two craft disappeared into the thick cloud cover, while the other gunship provided cover fire down below, swinging from one side of the mountaintop to the other.

Al Nichols and his brave crew took three more wounded men to a hospital, and like many who had gone before them, they all survived.

He was tired. All his crew members were tired. Everyone in Vietnam was tired. Soldiers were in a mad rush toward an end of a war that everybody knew they would not be allowed to win. Al and the rest could only keep trying to save as many lives as they could. They had to keep on trying tirelessly because Vietnam was a war of survival, and Al Nichols had the capability to help some people survive.

He was a character who came out of Special Forces. There were many such men, but they all had one thing in common. One single thread wove its way through each man's story: They were all men, and they were all heroes. I may not have been a hero myself, but I damned sure have been accused many times of being a character.

An army must be built on a sea of green, a large number of men and machines that will perform a job set out for them in specific written guidelines. Special Forces, however, was made up of individuals, mavericks who thought for themselves and prided themselves on their ability to always accomplish the mission. That and that alone is the ultimate in military leadership, and that is why Special Forces became so exclusive, so copied, so revered. They were the men of action, the best-trained fighting force the world has ever known. They were, and are, the ultimate in commandos, the ones you want when you have to win. They were the men of the Green Berets.

Epilogue

SPECIAL FORCES Major Jack E. "Happy Jack" Deckard retired from the U.S. Army and lived happily with his lovely wife Ruth and several beautiful daughters. He went into private business in Fayetteville, North Carolina, later returning to his native Missouri. There Jack became a successful real estate agent, but sadly he died from lung cancer several years ago. Ruth, his wife and companion of many years, was with him at the end, but Jack was back in Vietnam. Some might think that was nightmarish for him, but I choose to think it was wonderful. He was a warrior, and in his mind, I think, he was happy at what he did best. Jack was a friend who will be sorely missed. He was a man. He was SF.

Retired Lieutenant Colonel Alfred G. Nichols III now lives, as I do, in Canon City, Colorado, with his pretty wife and family. He retired from the Army on February 1, 1982, with more than twenty-four years of service. He is the senior army instructor of the Canon City High School ROTC program and is also a criminal justice instructor with Pueblo Community College. Additionally, he holds the rank of captain with the Canon City Police Reserves. He heads and trains the CCHS rifle team, which took first place in the state of Colorado last year. Like Al Fontes and myself, Al Nichols is also a member of Chapter XXIV, Special Forces Association in Colorado Springs.

Al Fontes has grown children and a pretty wife as well. He retired a command sergeant major after spending many years in SF and having a fine distinguished career. He not only belongs to the Special Forces Association, he was the founder of Chapter XXIV.

Kok Ksor and his beautiful wife H'li live in Spartanburg, South Carolina, and they still work tirelessly to make the world aware of the plight of their people. Besides being president of the FULRO, Kok created and heads the Montagnard Foundation, a nonprofit South Carolina corporation, set up to provide assistance to other Montagnards. Not only am I his senior adviser, but he and his wife, my wife, and I consider each other brothers and sisters. His sons, Thomas, Jonathan, Daniel, and John, all live at home and go to college. Kok speaks to veterans and other groups and Montagnards living in South Carolina.

Colonel Bob Kingston went on to command the JFK Special Warfare Center as a major general. After a distinguished military career as a four-star general, he and his lovely wife, Jo, finally retired to Alexandria, Virginia. There he has had several business interests and served important functions, such as when President Reagan sent him as a special negotiator to Hanoi with General Vessey. He has also been for many years the senior adviser on special operations to the director of the Central Intelligence Agency. My wife and I met with him a couple of years ago at the Tropicana Casino in Las Vegas and thoroughly enjoyed seeing him again.

I held the first-ever individual SF Vietnam A-team family reunion that I know of in Canon City, Colorado, during August 1992. I located some of the members of my A-team, Detachment A-242, Dak Pek, and they brought their families to Canon City. There we laughed, cried, played, and told lies to each other. Most of us were seeing each other for the first time since Vietnam, and our families got along as if they were all first cousins at a family reunion. It was wonderful, and we agreed to meet every two years. Our next reunion will be in Fort Lewis, Washington, in 1994.

In attendance were two of the survivors of the B-52 strike in Dak Pek, Tom Weeks and Commo Willy. Tom Weeks, after five Purple Hearts, a Silver Star, and twenty-seven years in the Army, retired as a command sergeant major and now works as a deputy sheriff in Olympia, Washington. There he lives with his wonderful and pretty wife Kyung and two of his children. Master Sergeant Don "Commo Willy" Williams, his pretty wife Terressa, and three ravishing daughters live in Wakeeney, Kansas. After more than four years straight in Vietnam, mostly at Dak Pek, twenty years in the Army, duty on the HALO and SCUBA Committees, Commo Willy was shot in the back in Lebanon and is now confined to a wheelchair, but he is still SF. The wheels simply became replacement legs for the tireless dynamo.

Colonel Joe Dietrich, our former team commander and my favorite CO ever, is still SF, serving with US-SOCOM at MacDill AFB in Florida. Another team CO, Jim Seders, retired from the Army reserves as a full colonel, too. He lives with his lovely wife Connie in Irving, Texas. Former sergeant Larry Vosen, and his beautiful wife and daughter, Charley and Andrea, own a restaurant in San Jose, California. Larry Crotsley, Dak Pek's former engineer/demolition NCO, owns a trucking company in New Jersey, where he is happily married to a beauty, Ilene, and they have two other beauties, Lauren and Megan. Retired Command Sergeant Joe Seyer and his lovely wife live in

Fayetteville, North Carolina, where Joe helps administer the national headquarters of the Special Forces Association. Steve Olson, retired master sergeant, and his pretty wife Carol live in Olympia, Washington, a mile from Tom Weeks. Steve has been the commander of a yacht and trailer club. Retired Command Sergeant Major Joe Kope and his gorgeous German-born wife Ila currently live in California, but like many SFers they have fun being a little nomadic.

Montagnard
Foundation, Inc.

Any reader wishing to make a tax-deductible contribution to the Montagnard Foundation, Inc., or write to Kok Ksor can do so by making checks payable or writing to:

Montagnard Foundation, Inc.
PO BOX 17064
Spartanburg SC 29301

The money you send is only used by and for Montagnards, for the betterment of Montagnards.

About the Author

Don Bendell was a captain in the U.S. Army Special Forces and served on an A-team in Vietnam in 1968 and 1969. At the time he lived with the Jeh tribe of Montagnards, and he still works with the Montagnards to this day as senior adviser to the president of the FULRO, the Montagnards' secret resistance movement fighting the racial discrimination levied against them by the Vietnamese government. He is active in the Special Forces Association, and he speaks to veterans' clubs and groups. He authored the very popular nonfiction Vietnam book *Crossbow,* and its more popular sequels *The B-52 Overture* and *Valley of Tears* (the latter two published by Dell).

Bendell is the author of the popular new *Chief of Scouts* series of Western novels, and he was nominated for two Spur awards.

Bendell wrote, produced, and directed the successful feature film *The Instructor.* A Sixth Degree Black Belt in tae kwon do, judo, and jujitsu, he has taught martial arts for two decades and is at the Master level. He is a senior member of the international board of directors of the World Martial Arts Council. In December 1992 he was inducted into the International Karate Hall of Fame.

Bendell is married and has two daughters and four sons. He enjoys tennis, golf, fishing, bowhunting, dancing, and horses.